D0127650

Washington Geographic Series

WASHINGTON
PORTRAIT OF THE LAND

BY ROBERT U. STEELQUIST

copyright © 1988
AMERICAN GEOGRAPHIC PUBLISHING
Helena, Montana

Text copyright © 1988
Robert U. Steelquist

WILLIAM A. CORDINGLEY, CHAIRMAN
RICK GRAETZ, PUBLISHER
MARK THOMPSON, DIRECTOR OF PUBLICATIONS
BARBARA FIFER, ASSISTANT BOOK EDITOR

This series provides in-depth information about Washington's geo-
graphic, natural history, historical and cultural subjects.
Design by Len Visual Design; Linda Collins, graphic artist. Printed in
Hong Kong by Nordica International Ltd.

To my parents—Davis R. Steelquist and Beverly Hansen Steelquist—who taught me to see history in the land.

Library of Congress Cataloging-in-Publication Data

Steelquist, Robert.
    Washington : portrait of the land / by Robert U. Steelquist.
        p.   cm. — (Washington geographic series ; no. 3)
        ISBN 0-938314-33-5 (pbk.) : $14.95
        1. Washington (State)—Description and travel. I. Title.
II. Series.
F891.S84 1988
917.97—dc19   88-994
                                CIP

ISBN 0-938314-33-5
© 1988 American Geographic Publishing
Box 5630, Helena, MT 59604
(406) 443-2842
Text © 1988 Robert U. Steelquist

ACKNOWLEDGMENTS

Washington: A Portrait of the Land has been an exciting and demanding project that would not have been possible without the gracious support from a long list of people. Mark Thompson has been very supportive through the book's frustrating times; his warmth and and patience are deeply appreciated. Barbara Fifer tamed my wild manuscript as only a Montana editor has courage to do.

I wish to thank Jo Ann Hughes of Peninsula College for expediting my interlibrary loan requests and stalling my overdue notices. Michael Hannan of Michael Hannan Books; Jim Catley of William James-Bookseller; David Hutchinson of Flora and Fauna Books; Bob DeWeese of Melville and Company and Sherburne Cook of Sherburne Antiques have all been helpful in locating useful, out-of-print reference books.

The interpretation of vegetational patterns that is reflected in the chapter on that subject is based extensively on the work of Jerry F. Franklin and C.T. Dyrness. I have taken the liberty of modifying their zone designations by using common names of important plant species instead of the Latin nomenclature. Dr. David Rice created an overview of Columbia Basin human prehistory by sharing his own work and that of Randall Schalk, James Chatters and Charles Borden. Dr. Rice also gave the chapter on prehistory a thoughtful review. Dr. Richard Daugherty and Dr. Carl Gustafson assisted in the gathering of photographs of excavations at the Manis and Marmes sites. Clare and Emanuel Manis granted permission to photograph Manis site objects. Eric Bergland gave critical advice in the interpretation of coastal prehistory.

Historic photographs were used from a variety of institutions. Thanks are due to Ed Nolan, Eastern Washington State Historical Society; Elizabeth Winroth, Oregon Historical Society; and Carolyn Marr, Museum of History and Industry. Some of the photographs used were located through the diligent efforts of Gail Evans and Karna Orsen. Laurel Black of Anaglyph Art Services created illustrations. I offer thanks to the photographers, particularly Pat O'Hara, Tom and Pat Leeson, Tore Ofteness and Karna Orsen.

My family—Jenny and Peter, Beverly Steelquist, and Ralph and Mildred Hall—and many friends, contributed moral support and mental relief during the months of this book's preparation. It is to them that I owe the deepest showing of gratitude.

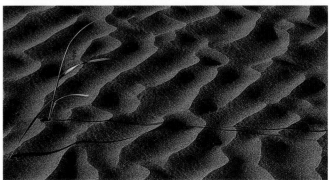

Left: *Phelps Creek drainage in the Glacier Peak Wilderness.* PAT O'HARA; **top:** *near the town of Starbuck.* PAT O'HARA; **bottom:** *sand patterns, Juniper Dunes Wilderness.* KEITH D. LAZELLE

Facing page, top left: *Alpine larch* KEITH D. LAZELLE; **top right:** *Starrett House, Port Townsend.* PAT O'HARA
Bottom: *Rhododendron, Washington's state flower.* ROBERT U. STEELQUIST

Cover photograph: *Valleys of the Olympic Peninsula filled with fog.* PAT O'HARA

Washington: Portrait of the Land

All history is natural history.

Left: Toleak Point in Olympic National Park.
Facing page: Pink and yellow monkeyflowers, Mt. Rainier National Park. PAT O'HARA PHOTOS

INTRODUCTION

From the rolling hills of the Palouse in spring to the broken headlands of the Pacific in summer; from the icy spires of Mt. Shuksan to the basalt cliffs of the Columbia Gorge, Washington is a mosaic of bold landscapes. In places, the surface of the land is recumbent, a smooth surface reflecting a uniform sheet of light. Elsewhere, the land is broken, scattering fragments of reflected light.

It is known as the Evergreen State, but it could be called the "every-green" state, for over the face of this land a welter of living things have found season. Forests mature in the deeper hues, like the blue-green of coastal spruce. The shrub-steppe plains of the Columbia Basin take on lighter shades—the silver-green of the common sage.

Washington: Portrait of the Land is a book about this place. It is about the land within a state within a nation; a place defined by its political boundaries; a physical landscape whose confines were originally created out of abstract values of strategy and political purpose. We seldom ponder the logic of those boundaries. Except where they coincide with lines of natural demarcation like the Columbia River or the Pacific Ocean, Washington's political boundaries have little to do with the stuff of terra firma.

This book is a geography of Washington. That concept is troublesome because it means many things to many people. Mention the word geography and a listener will conjure his or her own idea of the word that is necessarily broad. Some of us think of the school days image of pull-down maps decorated in bright colors—a world of time-zones, imports and exports, rivers and mountain ranges, numbers and capitals to tax the memory. Others think of the dusty stacks of *National Geographic* magazines in the basement or garage—a monthly journey to tribal hearth, volcanic caldera, ruins of ancient civilizations and the general ends of the earth that gives us intimate glimpses of places and people we are unlikely to encounter in person. Geography can be thought of as a subject of study or, in the case of the monthly journal, of entertainment—a ticket to the unfamiliar world at large, seen from the familiar comfort of an armchair.

The literary and scholarly heritage of a popular geography of a state is an American tradition that reaches back to 1787.

Frost-rimed cedar boughs.
JAMES RANDKLEV

Then, a former governor of Virginia, in response to queries from a French intellectual about his native region, published a collection of as many facts about Virginia as were within his grasp. The author, Thomas Jefferson, is better known for the radical political manifesto, the Declaration of Independence. His *Notes on the State of Virginia,* however, was the first attempt by a New World author to catalogue the climate, landforms, plants, animals and institutions in the fledgling nation. Jefferson betrayed his own far-flung curiosity in the scope of his book. Typical of the science of his day, he blended a host of disciplines (including geography) into what was called Natural Philosophy. In this context, a discourse on the rights of man was as appropriate as the measurement of Natural Bridge; a catalogue of important papers of state was as germane as a chapter on the distribution of Native American tribes, with a discussion of their languages. As we shall see, Jefferson's breadth of curiosity, revealed so well in *Notes on the State of Virginia,* would shape the study of other regions, including the one we now call Washington state. His was not just a descriptive art—it shaped the way the explorers of his day looked at the raw land of the West and saw in it the future.

Americans have always revelled in describing the American landscape—the more intimate the setting, the more intense the process. There is a pride in understanding a land from the perspective of one who lives with it—one who sees its moments, comprehends its scents, knows its distances in terms other than numbers. In my own varied travels throughout Washington, I have looked for the landscape that was seen by the early explorers, squinting to see past the built, and probing to find the natural. I have sought the landforms that figured in the imagination and tales of Native Americans. I have tried to see the natural tapestries of plant communities and the haunts of animals, reduced now by encroachment and disruption of man.

I have also sought clues to how this land has shaped humans—individuals, communities, economies and the future. As I have looked at Washington, I have measured my own impressions against a destiny shaped by the land itself. Are there clues in the gently flowing Columbia that tell us of the rise of an agricultural empire? Do ice-locked glacier fields of the Cascades hint at a state that will always be divided between dryside and wet? Is there such a thing as a determinism imposed by an unruly landscape?

I think the answers are all "yes." Yet in such an admission there is no defeat. We Washingtonians celebrate a vigorous land and a vigorous history. The variety of landscapes we encounter in our home state weaves the subtle explanation for the cultural diversity which is an equal source of our pride.

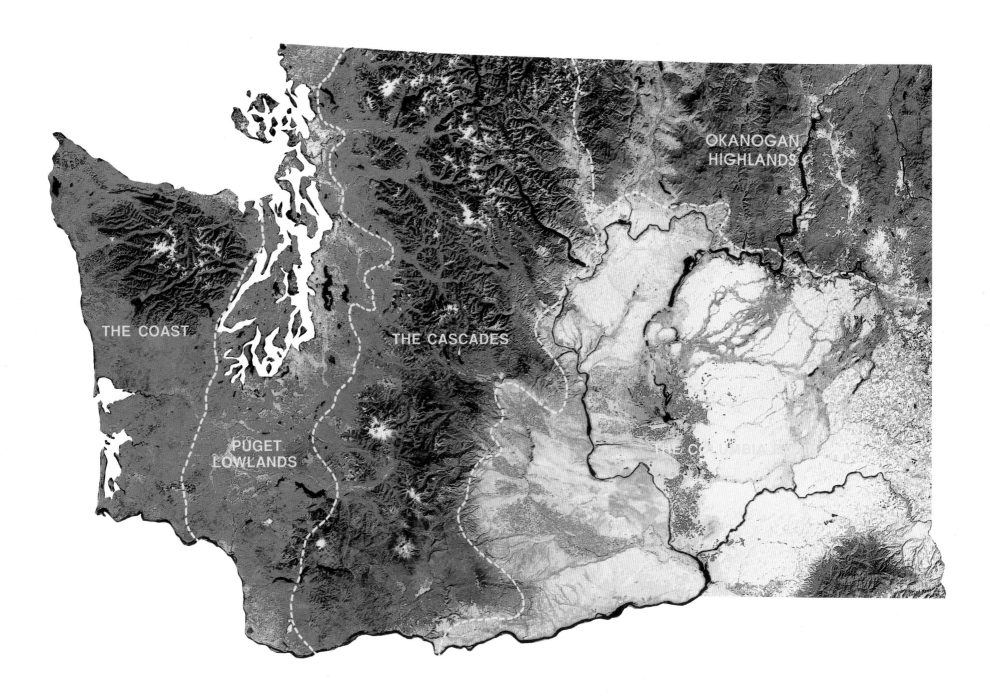

OKANOGAN
HIGHLANDS

THE COAST

THE CASCADES

PUGET
LOWLANDS

THE COLUMBIA

CHAPTER ONE

LANDFORMS

Above: *Basalt columns near Vantage.* PAT O'HARA

Right: *Autumn stillness along the Pend Orielle River.* JEFF GNASS

Facing page: *Mt. Rainier, Washington's loftiest peak.* PAT O'HARA

The wind buffets the bunchgrass relentlessly. Overhead, a kestrel trims its wings, delicately balancing itself between unseen layers of flowing air, momentarily achieving the grace of motionless suspense as it hangs like a kite in the sky. The blue-shadow lump of Mt. Rainier's summit overtops the Cascades to the west; the darkening sky is now the yellow-pink color of trout flesh. Below me sprawls the city of Yakima, lights twinkling on the outskirts and congealing toward downtown. No sounds emerge out of the valley—just the rush of wind. Atop the ridge the wrinkles and folds of this country smooth. The eye gathers in the far reaches of the Naches, the rolling hills to the east. Below, sprawling through the cottonwoods, the Yakima River flows south toward the hole of Union Gap. I ponder the gap. I know how it was formed: that the north-south run of the river predates the east-west rise of the ridge; that the rising land melted around the river like butter around a hot knife; that in the span of unknowable time such unthinkable things happen. Yet, in the press of the moment, a silent, motionless river appearing far below seems incapable of doing anything that would shape land, even in a time span of millions of years.

The evolution of Washington's landforms can be understood best in terms of three great themes of earth history: plate tectonics, volcanism and glaciation. Each is vividly displayed on a grand scale and together they account for much of the amazing array of landform features that characterize the state.

Plate tectonics

Our understanding of the evolution of the Washington landscape grew rapidly in the 1960s when the theory of plate tectonics gained broad acceptance among earth scientists. In Washington, as everywhere on the earth's face, this new conceptual framework helped assemble a single chronology of major continent-building events that occurred over millions of years. Whole regions can be characterized as markers along that chronology—a coherent record of a series of collisions which, in ages past, combined faraway landmasses with North America.

Plate tectonic theory established an account of several general mechanisms that have shaped and continue to shape the arrangement of the earth's surface. The theory envisions the earth's crust as a series of discrete rafts, or plates, floating on a dense liquid mantle. For millions of years, these rafts have shuffled around on the planet's surface, colliding, fusing and breaking apart. Present-day North America, for example, was connected recently (50 million years ago) to what is now Europe. Intense thermal activity within the earth weakened Pangaea, the former continent, and gradually formed a rift, or volcanic seam, deep beneath the ancient land mass. The rift grew in length as the halves began to move apart, and the Atlantic Ocean was born. As the rift widened, a new seafloor formed—the New World was moving slowly away from the Old.

The Atlantic rift revealed processes later seen in most of the ocean basins of the world. Its relatively thin crust of basalt is patterned with parallel ridges formed along the seam of the spreading ocean center. Rocks formed on these ridges bear magnetic fingerprints that can be used to accurately determine the position of the magnetic pole of the earth at the time the rocks crystallized following their submarine eruption. Ocean floor crust on either side of that seam moves in opposite directions, and the continents move farther apart as new molten material continually wells up along the rift.

The mechanisms seen in the Atlantic rift form a rather straightforward account of seafloor spreading. In the Pa-

cific Ocean, however, the scenario is more complex. The current spreading center of the Pacific is not located in a central position relative to the ocean basin itself. Rather, it is a mere 200 miles off the Washington coast and is being overtaken by movement of the North American plate. To further complicate matters, the eastern Pacific consists of several fragments of oceanic plates slipping past each other as they slip beneath the advancing edge of the continental margin in a process called *subduction*.

In the process of subduction, one plate is forced beneath the edge of another. As it is forced beneath another plate, the subducting plate is subjected to great pressure, and melts as it is swallowed in the earth's mantle. Subduction zones are the scenes of intense seismic and volcanic activity. In Washington, that activity is evident in the remains of episodes of past surface volcanic activity throughout the state as well as in the ongoing eruptions and activity of the young Cascades volcanoes.

Other evidence of subduction includes folded sediments that were formed as the continental shelf of the continental landmass. Deposited as relatively ordered layers of fine particles that have eroded off the land, sediments are compressed and tilted, often lifted thousands of feet above their former resting place beneath the sea. Washington state is striped with sedimentary rocks formed along what were at various times the edges of continental landmasses. The oldest of these form the limestones, sandstones and shales of the extreme northeastern part of the state. The youngest form the soft coastal bluffs of the Olympic Peninsula, where fossil clams and scallops of about 15 million years ago decorate the upturned boulders scattered at surf's edge.

The theory of how Washington's shaping began is described by David Alt and Donald Hyndman in their book, *Roadside Geology of Washington*. They outline a process in which several separate blocks, foreign to the North American continent, were plastered onto the leading edge of the westward-moving continent.

Rocks of North America's western shore, formed more than 300 million years ago, now are found along the extreme eastern boundary of Northern Washington. A broad continental shelf formed there as sediment flowed off the ancient continent and accumulated in the sea shallows. Movement of the continental plate gradually compressed the sedimentary rocks of the old continental shelf into a tightly folded mass now known as the Kootenay Arc. Sediments of the Kootenay Arc are visible in many locations including the Pend Oreille River Valley and near Colville and Kettle Falls.

The next piece of Washington moved into place about 100 million years ago, according to Alt and Hyndman. This piece consisted of a small continent that collided with North America, the remnants of which now form the Okanogan highlands. The Okanogan subcontinent is bordered on the west with sedimentary remnants of its western continental shelf and subduction trench. Sedimentary rocks in the Okanogan Valley represent the contents of the old subduction trench that was deformed and compressed by the addition of another foreign landmass that followed.

About 50 million years after the Okanogan subcontinent docked, the conveyor belt of moving oceanic crust delivered another continental mass to North America's western shore—the North Cascades subcontinent. The North Cascades subcontinent is thought to have traveled considerable distance before its collision with North America. Fossil evidence suggests that many of the sediments originally were deposited in a tropical environment. In addition, the continent was relatively mature in its own right. Its core consisted of rocks that had undergone considerable alteration by heat and pressure while it still was far from North America. Rocks of this crystalline core are visible today in parts of the North Cascades, where they appear as streaky puddings of pressure-altered granites and sedimentary rocks.

During its collision with North America, the North Cascades subcontinent endured powerful straining forces in which western portions of the tectonic assemblage were driven northward. This resulted in a series of fault lines that run along a north-south axis through the North Cascades. According to Alt and Hyndman, displacement of rocks on either side of the Straight Creek fault may exceed 100 miles. Sedimentary rocks of what was formerly the continental shelf on the west coast of the North Cascades subcontinent now are found in the western foothills of the North Cascades, disappearing beneath the accumulation of glacial debris of the Puget Trough.

Washington's coast ranges, the Olympic Mountains and Willapa Hills, are newcomers to the Washington landscape. The Olympics form the mountainous core of the Olympic Peninsula, rising to nearly 8,000' of elevation within a relatively short distance from salt water. Water

and glaciers have gnawed voraciously at the young range, producing some of Washington's most scenic landforms. At the heart of the range is Mt. Olympus (7,965'), which is made of sandstone and shale that have been heavily warped and buckled.

The Olympics are intensely deformed and eroded remnants of a subduction trench that was forced against the edge of the advancing continent and tilted into its present position by the slow impact of the subduction process. As sediments flowed off the western slope of the continent, they gathered into great sheets on the ocean floor. Interbedded formations of basalt and other debris from submarine volcanic eruptions appear—some younger, some older than the sediments. As the relatively light sediments collided with the advancing edge of the continent, they pitched upward and were subjected to intense fracturing. Signs of distortion of both grand and minute scale in the original beds are found throughout the

The Palouse River tumbles over layers of Columbia Basalt at Palouse Falls.

Facing page: *Sandstone shores of Matia Island bathed in sunset light. Mt. Baker and the Twin Sisters in the distance.* PAT O'HARA PHOTOS

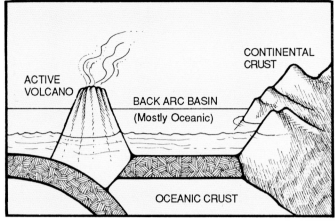

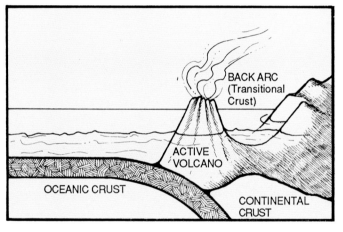

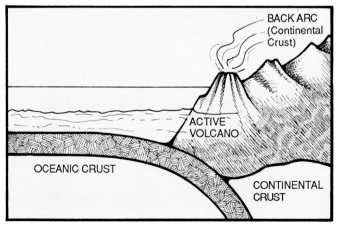

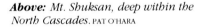
Above: *Mt. Shuksan, deep within the North Cascades.* PAT O'HARA

Right: *Geologists believe that Washington's mountain ranges were formed as a sequence of crustal blocks collided with the North American continent.* LAUREL BLACK

Olympics. Great folds are seen in rock formations, and localized bedding structures reveal formerly ordered beds of slate shattered into fine shards known as "slate pencils."

Volcanism

The serene appearance of the great Cascade peaks on a clear day belies the fury that shaped much of the Washington landscape. Volcanism, in its various forms, has produced not only most of the peaks of Washington, but its greatest plain as well—the Columbia Plateau.

Washington is located along one of the most celebrated zones of volcanism on earth, the Pacific Rim of Fire. From Tierra del Fuego to New Zealand, the convergence of tectonic plates drives an internal fury that creates mountain ranges and island arcs. Any resident of the Pacific Northwest on May 18, 1980, the day that Mt. St. Helens exploded, can attest to the suddenness and might of an active volcano.

Of Washington's eight highest mountain peaks, seven are volcanic in their origin. These are Columbia Crest (14,410′) and Little Tahoma (11,117′) on Mt. Rainier; Mt. Adams (12,276′); Glacier Peak summit (10,541′) and

Disappointment Peak (9,755') on Glacier Peak; and Grant (10,788') and Sherman (10,133') peaks on Mt. Baker. Each of Washington's great volcanoes is classified as a *stratovolcano,* composed of alternate layers of ash, lava and mud that succumb rapidly to glacial erosion. The Cascade volcanoes are young. The present peaks have appeared on the scene within the last 25,000 years. In addition, each of the volcanoes shows signs of numerous eruptions—overlapping summit cones, layers of rock that vary in composition and telltale ash layers spewed over thousands of square miles, often at a great distance from their volcanic source. Each mountain has been aggressively eroded by glacial action, its smooth, youthful appearance gouged and broken by massive rivers of ice that have attended to the destruction of the mountain since the instant of its birth.

In addition to the snowcapped volcanoes that mark the current volcanic period, other periods of volcanism created older ranges that have long since eroded. As the North Cascades subcontinent neared the continent prior to its docking, the subduction process fueled volcanoes near the old continental edge. Massive deposits of andesite and rhyolite are now found in the Sanpoil River valley. These deposits were the product of eruptions caused by the approach of the North Cascade subcontinent and the underthrusting of ocean crust that separated subcontinent from continent. More recent volcanic events formed much of the foundation upon which the present Southern Cascades peaks rest. Andesite flows of the Ohanapecosh formation are visible from the Columbia River Gorge north to Enumclaw.

The Columbia Plateau bears signs of a form of volcanism that is very poorly understood. General agreement exists, however, that the eruptions responsible for the flood basalts of the Columbia Plateau were among the greatest outpourings of magma known. Approximately 15 million years ago, a series of eruptions poured highly fluid magma from open vents and covered a region in excess of 200,000 square miles. Moving at an estimated speed of 25 to 30 miles per hour, the magma spread over the relatively gentle topography, with later flows adding many layers to the overall formation. Near the center of the flow region, basalt exceeds 10,000' in thickness. The many-columned rimrock that lines the Columbia River near Vantage is characteristic of the structure of the Columbia Basalt. Five- and six-sided

columns appear neatly stacked against one another along miles of dark escarpments. Individual flows are evident as distinct layers in the columnar structure. The source vents of these basalts are thought to be located in the vicinity of the extreme southeastern corner of Washington, although not all authorities agree on this point.

Not all volcanic activity driven by the engine of subduction results in surface volcanic activity. Magma generated by deep volcanism often remains trapped within the continent. Such bodies are referred to as batholiths and plutons. These formations cool slowly, forming massive bodies of relatively homogeneous rock such as granite. The force of a large quantity of magma being injected into a landmass can result in broad uplifting. In addition, the heat of an intrusive body alters the surrounding rock, often resulting in the formation of ores. Some of Washington's most spectacular mountain landscapes are formed by the exposure of batholiths and plutons as the softer surrounding rock has eroded away. Examples include the Kettle Range and Mt. Spokane in northeastern Washington, the Golden Horn batholith near Washington Pass, the Stuart batholith north of Ellensburg and the Tatoosh pluton, which forms the footing for Mt. Rainier.

Basalt columns of the Columbia Plateau reveal the slow cooling of great sheets of molten basalt lava that spread over much of eastern Washington about 15 million years ago.
PAT O'HARA

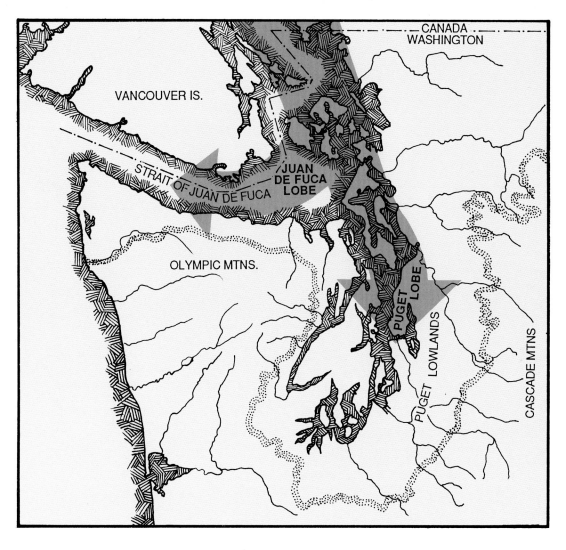

The Puget Lowlands and Strait of Juan de Fuca were gouged by two lobes of glacial ice that visited the region during the last Ice Age. The shaded line shows the extent of glaciation.
LAUREL BLACK

Glaciation

Washington State contains some of the world's most accessible glaciers, enabling scientists and casual observers alike to view the processes that have shaped much of the Washington landscape. From the radiant mantle of ice on Mt. Rainier to the remote icefields of the North Cascades, glaciers continuously gnaw into the mountains.

Active glaciers in Washington are known as *alpine* glaciers. They are restricted to mountainous regions of the Cascade and Olympic ranges, where a combination of factors including elevation, slope and climate influences their growth and shrinkage in a finely tuned balance. Approximately 950 glaciers dot Washington's mountain landscapes, with a total surface area of 162 square miles. Washington ranks behind only Alaska in glaciated area among the states. Washington's glaciers represent a vast water storage capacity, and are very important in regulating the flow of water from the mountains to the lowlands.

The heavy hand of glacial erosion and deposition has left its mark over much of the lowland. In the last million years, several episodes of continental or *cordillerian* glaciation radically rearranged the Puget Sound lowland. These events were in response to major climatic variations felt everywhere on earth. During these ice ages, the overall distribution of water on the planet's surface shifted. As temperatures dropped, water became locked in vast ice caps and valley glacier systems of the mountain ranges. Sea level dropped.

The most recent cordillerian event—called the Fraser Glaciation because the major ice flow moved south through what is now the Fraser River valley of British Columbia—occurred between 15,000 and 12,000 years ago. One vast lobe advanced southward in the trough between the Olympic Mountains and the Cascades. It dammed river valleys that drained the western Cascades and diverted all of the westward-flowing rivers south of what is now Puget Sound through the Chehalis River Valley and into the Pacific. Much of the Puget lowland now is covered with a thick blanket of sand, gravel and silt—material that originally formed the mountain ranges of British Columbia.

Alpine glaciers also grew dramatically during the Fraser Glaciation. The narrow U-shaped basins of Lake Chelan and the Methow Valley are examples of the erosive power of the vast rivers of ice. Major river valleys throughout Washington bear moraines and kame terraces, which are large deposits of gravel heaped around the glacier as it occupied a valley and later dumped when the glacier wasted.

Perhaps the most astonishing remnant of the ice age in Washington is the broad region in the Columbia Basin known as the Channeled Scablands. The scablands are the result of a flood unleashed as continental glaciers melted following the last major continental glacial event. Ice dams had created vast lakes in the interior basins of

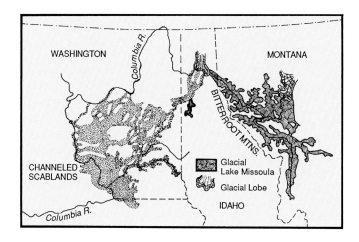

the Rocky Mountains. Warming conditions caused failure of the dams and the release the largest surges of floodwater known from earth history. Estimates of the total amount of water that poured over the Columbia Plateau run between 50 and 500 cubic miles of water—all coursing to the Pacific in a period of about two weeks. The boiling floods carved the Grand Coulee and many other features in a region larger than 12,000 square miles. One feature, now known as Dry Falls, was a thundering cataract that moved headward nearly seven miles as flood torrents eroded the basalt bedrock.

As the modern climate evolved following the last Ice Age, the land as we see it now began to take its form. Sea level rose, drowning the lower reaches of glacier-influenced valleys including the Puget Sound basin and Grays Harbor. The Columbia River returned to its bed, skirting the edge of the basalt flows in a great bend to the west, southwest and east. Floodways of the Spokane Floods were abandoned, deeper basins were left containing lakes such as Moses Lake, and scabland channels carrying small streams such as Crab Creek and Cow Creek. River systems stabilized, and occupied the channels that they had inherited. Where rivers adopted broad, flat-bottomed valleys shaped by glaciers, the rivers have had full play, looping and bending, carving new channels and abandoning old ones. Glacial valleys have benefited from such riverine wanderlust, however, because they have accumulated deep mantles of bottomland soil.

Above: *Glaciers chew into the flanks of Whatcom Peak. Mt. Blum looms beyond the knife-edge crest of Easy Ridge.*
Left: *Mt. Olympus and the Blue Glacier from High Divide, Olympic National Park.* PAT O'HARA PHOTOS
Drawing, top left: *A series of catastrophic floods scoured Eastern Washington during the last Ice Age. Originating in the broad valleys of western Montana, floodwaters produced Washington's distinctive "Channeled Scablands."* LAUREL BLACK

CHAPTER TWO

CLIMATE & VEGETATION

Above: *Petrified wood: a snapshot of vegetation and climate millions of years ago.* FRANK S. BALTHIS
Right: *Western larch, aflame in the cool heat of a sunlit autumn day* JEFF GNASS

There is no thought nor hope of rain during the summer, and our traveller, fretting under manifold discomforts, cannot find words strong enough to express his disgust and disappointment. Even an approach to the majestic Columbia brings no relief, for its low banks are verdureless to the water's edge. After it has been crossed and left behind there is no apparent change for the better in the succeeding hundred miles. To be sure, there is another river to be seen after a while, and the dust-enveloped train seems to be following its course; but the glare and heat are unabated, while on both sides the sage-brush still flaunts its ashen-hued mockery of foliage.

Kirk Monroe, describing the Columbia Basin
Harper's Weekly, 1894

The whole country, up to the perpetual snow, is covered with a gigantic forest of evergreen trees, consisting of fir, spruce and cedar. On the American side, the forest appears jagged and uneven; dead trees rising like departed giants above the green foliage of the living, give rather repulsive appearance to the scene....The stupendous nature of this scenery can be conceived of, when a forest growth of trees a hundred feet high are by comparison with the lofty peaks above them, made to appear as if they were but grass, covering the surface of the earth.

James Swan, describing the Strait of Juan de Fuca
San Francisco Evening Bulletin, 1859

Visitors to Washington always have commented on the mantle of living substance that covers the land. Not surprisingly, both of the observers quoted above betray certain discomfort with the appearance of the natural vegetation here. Washington, in its extremes of lushness and barrenness, displayed a wildness unsettling to pioneer sensibilities. Today, Washington's capacity to produce plantlife under the nurturing hand of man is world-renowned. Here are some of the most productive forests, orchards and wheatlands on earth.

General characteristics of Washington weather patterns are due to the state's position slightly north of halfway between the equator and the north pole. As a result, there is significant seasonal variation in temperature and day length, as well as in general patterns of high- and low-pressure systems over the region. Washington sits astride a mid-latitude cyclonic storm belt. Shifts in high-pressure masses over the northeastern Pacific result in variations in the storm-belt path across Washington. When summer high-pressure masses hang over the ocean, winds generally blow from the northwest, skies are cloudless and temperatures warm. During winter months, low-pressure systems typically occupy the offshore region. Winds originate in the southwest and accompany considerable precipitation and cool temperatures. The general pattern of moist winters and dry summers is common throughout Washington, although the landform characteristics of the state have a considerable effect in shaping more localized conditions.

Washington's most profound climatic diversity results from the Cascade Range, which forms an effective barrier to moisture-laden maritime air moving inland. The damp Pacific air is forced upward over the rising topography and into cooler layers of the atmosphere. This results in condensation of water vapor into droplets of water or, when the surrounding air is cold enough, into crystals of snow or ice. The typical pattern of a maritime climate occurs, with abundant precipitation on one side of the Cascades and a continental climate with significantly less precipitation on the other, in the mountains' "rainshadow." The stark difference between the west side of the mountains, parts of which may receive as much as 150″ of precipitation annually, and the parched east side, where certain localities receive as little as 10″ annually, gives rise to much of the diversity of Washington's natural habitats, agricultural capabilities and other commercial and cultural factors that characterize the state's regional identities.

The soft mat of the ponderosa forest floor. PAT O'HARA

Although the dominant climatic theme of Washington state can be viewed in terms of East and West, localized variation of landforms creates odd juxtapositions within each of the broad regions. West of the Cascades, the rainshadow effect of the Olympic Mountains results in the semi-arid conditions found along the eastern Strait of Juan de Fuca and throughout the San Juan Islands. Here, annual precipitation varies between 12″ and 20″, making this the driest coastal area north of San Diego County, California. In addition, low-elevation forests northwest of Mt. Rainier receive greater rainfall than elsewhere in the Puget Lowland. Although a considerable distance inland, these forests bear striking resemblances to coastal "rain forest" environments of the Olympic Peninsula, an area known as

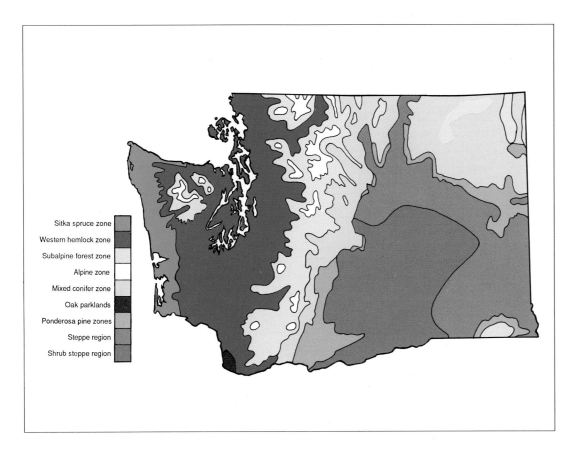

Above: *Washington is a mosaic of vegetation patterns that reflect its differing climates, soils and other factors of a diverse environment.*
LAUREL BLACK

Facing page: *Beargrass on Salmo Mountain. South-facing slopes in the Selkirk Mountains reveal a history of wildfire and slow regeneration typical of high-elevation forests.*
GEORGE WUERTHNER

Legend:
- Sitka spruce zone
- Western hemlock zone
- Subalpine forest zone
- Alpine zone
- Mixed conifer zone
- Oak parklands
- Ponderosa pine zones
- Steppe region
- Shrub steppe region

the wettest in Washington. East of the Cascades, the west-facing slope of the Selkirk Range, a portion of the Rockies extending into the extreme northeast corner of the state, receives annual precipitation comparable to areas of western Washington. And within the range itself, particularly in the North Cascades where the mountain belt is widest, weather pockets similar to either general climatic pattern can be found in specific adjacent localities.

The current climate regime—moist in the west, semi-arid in the east—is geologically recent. The rise of the Cascade Range as we know it occurred within the last 10 million years. Unfortunately, because conditions that allow the preservation of fossils were not as common in the Washington Cascades as in other places, the fossil record of the climate changes of this period is limited. One area of Washington that has revealed a wealth of information about forests of an earlier period is found along what is

now the eastern slope of the Cascades. The Ginkgo Petrified Forest apparently represents an area that was lushly forested about 15 million years ago with a wide assortment of coniferous and deciduous trees. Formed during the interval of Columbia Flood basalts, petrified wood-bearing deposits consist of sedimentary rocks formerly sealed between layers of the flood basalts. The remarkable quality of the preserved remains is due to the unique physical and chemical conditions of their burial.

Forests of Western Washington

The most superficial examination of the natural productions of Washington Territory cannot fail to show that it possesses a remarkable variety of botanical and zoological regions, each distinguished by more or less peculiar forms of life.

J.G. Cooper, M.D.
Naturalist, Pacific Railroad Surveys, 1853

Prior to the arrival of white settlers, forests occupied most of the land between saltwater and timberline. Although broken by scattered prairies, some of which were maintained by Indians through periodic burning, much of lowland western Washington was covered with dense forest consisting of Douglas fir, western hemlock and western red cedar. Although remarkably homogeneous in appearance, the maritime forests of Washington reveal considerable diversity.

Along the coast, the Sitka Spruce Zone is characterized by mild climate with high precipitation. Annual rainfall frequently exceeds 80". Summer drought is moderated by coastal fog—condensation in the needles of the trees contributes moisture even in the absence of rainfall. Soils are acidic and contain large quantities of organic material. Although Sitka spruce is considered the dominant tree species, western hemlock, western redcedar and Douglas fir are very common. River banks and other disturbed sites contain significant stands of red alder.

One distinctive variant within the Sitka Spruce Zone is the "Olympic rainforest." Tucked in the valleys of the Hoh, Queets, Quinault Rivers among the western foothills of the Olympic Mountains, these lush stands form some of the most productive temperate forests known. Trees grow to mammoth proportion, frequently reaching above 200' in height, with bases measuring as much as 10' in diameter. Hardwood species, including vine maple and bigleaf maple, sport thick coats of moss, clubmoss and fern. These epiphytes absorb and hold considerable quantities of moisture and airborne nutrients, forming a second soil that the trees exploit to aid their own growth.

The forest zone that includes most of lowland western Washington is called the Western Hemlock Zone. The enormous productivity of forests of this region was responsible for the emergence of Washington as a principal timber producer. And because of their obvious economic importance, these forests have been the subject of innumerable studies. In spite of the widespread presence of Douglas fir and western redcedar, western hemlock is considered the dominant species because of its tolerance for shade. Douglas fir requires significant disturbance such as fire, windstorm or clearcutting in order to reseed and grow. Western hemlock, on the other hand, can sustain its presence in the mature forest with ongoing recruitment to the stand. Western redcedar is a significant associate in moist sites such as stream corridors and ravines.

The Western Hemlock Zone is characterized by moderate temperature, abundant winter precipitation and relatively dry summers. Trees attain massive size in old-growth stands, their mighty boles rising as pillars supporting a vaulted canopy. Old-growth forests are complex structural and ecological environments that support a wide variety of invertebrates and fungi as well as higher plants and animals. In second-growth stands, Douglas fir often is more abundant than western hemlock or cedar, due to its aggressive pioneering habit following disturbance. Hemlock and cedar gradually reassert their presence, however, because of their ability to regenerate beneath the closed canopy.

Distinctive localized forest types are found within the Western Hemlock Zone throughout the Puget Sound region. These include oak parklands and open stands of lodgepole pine. These communities can be partially attributed to excessively drained soils overlying glacial outwash and course drift and locally dry climatic regimes.

Lowland forests west of the Cascades occasionally break into other habitats—a relief from the closed quietness of the evergreen canopy. Throughout the Puget Trough, prairies and bogs, which are geologic remnants of Ice Age inundation, are maintained by a variety of ecological mechanisms. Areas where glaciers rubbed the bedrock clear of a soil mantle, where deep glacial deposits of fast-draining gravel formed excessively porous soils and where large ice blocks created kettles or pools in the surrounding

Above: *Temperate rainforests of the western Olympic Peninsula represent the northern hemisphere's most productive forest ecosystems.*
PAT O'HARA

Right: *Arrowleaf balsamroot, a showy wildflower of eastern Washington's arid rangelands.*
CINDY McINTYRE

Facing page: *Vast stands of stately conifers dominate western Washington's mid-elevation forests.*
PAT O'HARA

glacial deposits, all comprise distinctive habitats that resisted forestation.

The rainshadow effect of the Olympic Mountains causes drought over much of the San Juan Islands, the northeast Olympic Peninsula and Whidbey Island. Barren rock outcrops in the San Juans now sport cactus, oak and other plantforms that manage to thrive under drought conditions. Natural prairies dotted much of this region when white settlers arrived. The Sequim prairie, an oak savannah sprinkled with Douglas fir invaders, ceased to exist as a unique habitat when irrigation ditch seepage altered the groundwater regime. Other prairie remnants, including a tiny fragment under protective management in Port Townsend, host camas, beargrass and a score of other prairie plants that have vanished elsewhere in their lowland range as urbanization and agriculture increased.

Peat bogs, filling with organic debris since the Ice Age and staving off forest growth because of their acidity and excessive moisture, are sprinkled throughout the lowland region. When excavated systematically, these bogs yield records of past climates and lifeforms in the form of pollen, trapped among the layers of peat. This record has been very useful in establishing a chronology of wet and dry spells and the resulting patterns of vegetation that covered Western Washington between the wasting of the great glaciers and the present.

Mid-elevation forests of Western Washington are described by Franklin and Dyrness as the Pacific Silver Fir Zone. Extending from between about 2,000′ and 3,000′ to about 4,200′ in elevation, this zone is cool and moist, receiving much of its annual precipitation in the form of snow. In Washington, the zone is dryer in the Southern

Cascades than in the North Cascades and Olympics. Associates of the silver fir include western hemlock, redcedar and Douglas fir in moist areas and Douglas fir and western white pine in drier areas. Understory shrubs frequently consist of salal, huckleberry and devil's club. Silver fir forests are relatively uncommon in the rainshadow portion of the Olympics, where mid-elevation forests are largely composed of western hemlock and Douglas fir. Where isolated stands of silver fir are encountered in this area, they usually are associated with localized cold pockets.

Subalpine areas of Western Washington range from about 4,200′ to 5,500′ in the north, and 4,100′ to 6,000′ in the south and are referred to by Franklin and Dyrness as the Mountain Hemlock Zone. Moister sites with old-growth stands are dominated by mountain hemlock. Drier locations, particularly those subject to disturbance such as the eastern timberline areas of the eastern Olympics and Southern Cascades, are dominated by subalpine fir with understory communities of huckleberry and beargrass. Other common tree species include lodgepole pine and whitebark pine, which often appear in pure stands, and Alaska cedar, which appears in moist ravines and avalanche tracks. Subalpine forests typically break into extensive meadow areas near timberline, clustering in small stands where moisture is conserved in lingering shaded snowpatches. Fog drip, the condensation of moisture from humid air into the cold needles, contributes significant moisture during the summer, even when rain is lacking.

At timberline, the upper edge of the world that trees can successfully reign over, treeforms assume the contorted shapes that reveal extreme environmental conditions and the plants' physiological limits. Trees appear in the bent, sprawling habit known as *krummholz* (German for "bent wood"), either wind-flagged or as cushions, and frequently bear scars or show exposed wood that has been "sandblasted" free of bark by windblown ice crystals. Where trees assume a conical form that allows them to readily shed snow loads, broad skirts—long limbs that are covered and insulated by overlying snow—may flank the trees' bases.

Eastern Forests

Crossing the Cascade summit by way of any of the major passes one immediately becomes aware of the

transition between Washington's moist and dry regions. Often, the overcast that has enveloped the western slope vanishes. The warmer hues of open land appear in the distance. The forests thin and pine appears. Indeed, the forests of Eastern Washington are a strong indicator that one has just crossed into a territory where profoundly different conditions order the scheme of living things.

Forests of Eastern Washington are constrained powerfully by climate—to the extent that there are actually two timberlines denoting the boundaries of the forest zones. One, the upper timberline, is a vivid representation of a complex set of interactions centered around cold. The other, the lower timberline, is determined by interactions associated with drought. Between these two striking frontiers, trees as dominant lifeforms claim their foothold over the land.

The most widespread forest zones of Eastern Washington are the Douglas Fir and Grand Fir zones, which occupy the mid-elevation mountainous regions. These are areas of moderate moisture regimes, particularly in terms of soil moisture content. The Douglas Fir Zone dominates the northern part of the region; the Grand Fir Zone includes the Southern Cascades. The Douglas Fir Zone, extending from about 1,900' to 4,200', supports, in addition

to its namesake, a varying mix of ponderosa pine, lodgepole pine and western larch. The Grand Fir Zone occupies slightly higher elevations, and displays a mix dominated by grand fir, but also includes ponderosa pine, lodgepole pine, western larch and Douglas fir.

Higher-elevation sites of the eastern forests consist of western hemlock and western redcedar between 2,600' and 4,000' and subalpine fir, whitebark pine, alpine larch and mountain hemlock between a lower boundary of 4,200' to 5,500' and the upper boundary, timberline, which varies from 6,000' to 8,000'.

Bordering the lower timberline is the Ponderosa Pine Zone. East of the Cascades, it forms a relatively narrow, uniform band between nine and 18 miles wide, opening into broad expanses through the Okanogan Highlands and the Blue Mountains. This forest consists of open stands of widely-spaced trees, frequently with understory populations of bunchgrass and sage. Quaking aspen frequently appears along stream corridors or in damp meadows. The zone correlates with the Arid Transition Zone of the Merriam Life-Zone System. Average annual precipitation within the Ponderosa Pine Zone is between 14" and 30".

Eastern Grasslands

Perhaps the most distinctive vegetational province of Eastern Washington is one that appears, at first glance, largely devoid of life—the desert of the Columbia Basin. Failing the usual test of vegetative opulence (the presence of forests), this region has been largely underappreciated as a living landscape. As a result, much of it has been subjected to reclamation or chronic overgrazing. But remnants of the original bunchgrass steppe and shrub/grass sagelands reveal complex interactions and surprising vitality.

Basing their opinion primarily on the pioneering work of plant ecologist Rexford Daubenmire, Franklin and Dyrness characterize Eastern Washington native grasslands under two broad categories: steppe and shrub steppe. Steppe environments typically are grasslands dominated by perennial bunchgrasses such as bluebunch wheatgrass and Idaho fescue. Shrub steppes are dominated by common or tall sage, with bunchgrasses and other plants occupying the understory. In broader geographic terms, the steppe region occupies much of the area characterized by the Palouse Hills, gently rolling terrain with deep aeolian (wind-deposited) soils. Shrub steppe occupies the drier regions of the central Columbia Basin. Although described in terms of their most conspicuous plantforms, both steppe and shrub steppe environments offer a profusion of herbs, grasses and shrubs including wild sunflower, arrowleaf balsamroot, rose, snowberry, lupine, paintbrush, bitterbrush and many others.

The region as a whole has been transformed by agriculture. In place of rolling hills of bunchgrass, the deep fertile soils of the Palouse now support some of the richest wheatlands known. Within the reach of the Columbia Basin Irrigation Project, sagebrush—long considered the true measure of worthlessness—has given way to lush fruit orchards, vineyards and vegetable fields, the universal measures of worth. Throughout the region, decades of sheep- and cattle-grazing have left a tracery of footpaths and the telltale blush of springtime cheatgrass imprinted on the rolling hillsides. Desert and garden, Washington's arid grasslands rival its verdant forests in symbolizing the diversity and promise of the land that westering man encountered, and which became Washington state.

CHAPTER THREE

NATIVE CULTURES

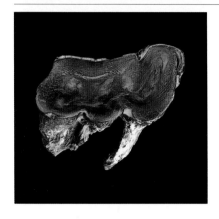

Above: *A worn tooth from a mastodon. This mastodon appears to have been butchered, suggesting the activity of early man at the end of the Ice Age, about 12,000 years ago. Manis site, Sequim.* KARNA ORSEN

Right: *Settlement patterns in the east came and went with climate change and mostly followed a narrow strip along the Columbia River and its tributaries. This is the view from the Oregon side of the Wenaha River to the Wenaha-Tucannon Wilderness of the Blue Mountains.* GEORGE WUERTHNER

Facing page: *Hobuck Beach on Mukkaw Bay, Makah Indian Reservation.* JEFF GNASS

Written history of Washington begins with the arrival of Europeans via the sea—mariners set on discovery and commerce. It continued with the overland arrival of fur traders, whose goal was lucrative commerce in animal skins. In each case, the written works were fragmentary accounts, disjointed in both time and space. They represented glimpses of strange landscapes and "new" plants and animals, caught in the moment of the voyager's brief stay, static frames intended to represent for the world and all time the features of an unfolding country. In retrospect, the early recorded history of Washington is like a collection of pot shards, broken and incomplete. Yet, glimpses emerge consistently through the accounts of the native people—their broad dispersion, their elaborate material cultures, their cosmopolitan trade economies and their various means of subsistence in an environment rich in resource diversity.

What Euro-Americans discovered when they arrived in the Northwest was that the land already had been "discovered," that the minutest details of the natural world had been mastered and integrated into the day-to-day activities of human societies. In addition, the relationship was known on another level, that of the psyche or spirit. The entire fabric of the cosmos was accounted for; the fullness of the world was known and connections were traced among its constituent parts.

Certainly, to European eyes, such an expression of humanity fell far below the standards they used to gauge human achievement. But the newcomers nevertheless were astounded by the sophistication of the material cultures, the precision with which the natives understood their world, and the art and ritual that they used to express their place in it. So too were whites impressed with the worldliness of the Indians as trading partners. While Indian goods generally could be obtained at terms generous to whites, centuries of intertribal commerce had established a tradition of shrewdness. And finally, where the European or American was at his weakest—knowledge of the land itself and the need for fresh stores of food—whites availed themselves to each scrap of knowledge of the country and each morsel that the natives were willing to offer. Overlanders particularly relied upon the native inhabitants to guide them, their success not so much dependent on their educated sense of direction as on the advice given by native informants.

Many Languages and a Universal One

The far-flung bands of Indians that whites first encountered represented a diverse range of linguistic and cultural traditions that bridged the vast differences in the Northwest landscape itself. Anthropologists now categorize Indian languages of North America into three broad families: Amerind, Na-Dene and Eskimo-Aleut. The families represent areas with the broadest geographical extent, and probably represent three discrete movements of humans over the Bering land bridge at separate times during and after the Pleistocene.

The earliest migration is thought to correspond with the spread of Amerind, which pervades the broadest geographical range in North and South America and exhibits the highest degree of subsequent differentiation. The second migratory wave, represented by Na-Dene, is geographically less diffuse and linguistically more compact. The third, Eskimo-Aleut, represents the most recent migration. It is geographically the most confined and, even today, retains close linguistic affinity to languages of Siberia.

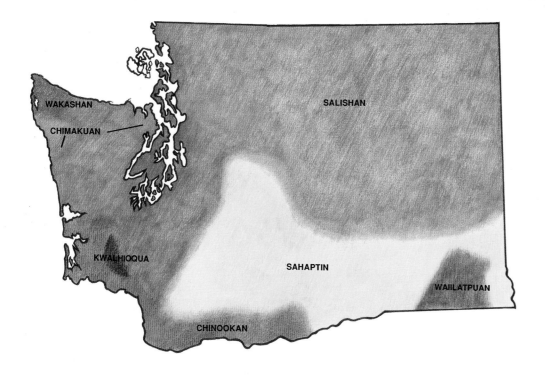

Native language families.
LAUREL BLACK

the original Chinook language in that it derived many words from Wakashan and other language groups. With the jargon, tribes of the coast traded among themselves (Nootka Indians from Vancouver Island possessed the greatest resources of marine invertebrates for shell money; Chinooks brokered slaves) and with interior tribes by way of the mountain passes and the great corridor of the Columbia River. The later addition of English and French words expanded the jargon dramatically, and admitted Europeans and Americans into the trading process. The very presence of the jargon, however, testifies to the importance of the geographical, linguistic and cultural nexus of the region now called Washington.

In Washington, the jargon enabled the direct and indirect mingling of Northwest Coast cultures with those of the Great Plains and Great Basin. Eastern Washington tribes in turn mixed freely with buffalo and horse cultures of the Rocky Mountain front. Coastal tribes traded with the potlatch and canoe Indians of Vancouver and the Queen Charlotte Islands, sharing traditions of ritual and subsistence common to inhabitants of the maritime regions. And within Washington, those diverse influences met at mountain passes, falls on the rivers and elsewhere in a lively trade economy that flourished.

Cultures Shaped by the Coast

It was in the material cultures of Washington Indians that the ultimate fit between human society and environment was demonstrated. The land and its resources shaped the societies, the cycles of season established the rhythms of village and hunt life, the lengths of drought and depths of snowfall determined the rise and fall of good fortune and the collective urge to move on or to stay. In the produce of the land were food and the materials for every made object.

Students of human prehistory of the Pacific Northwest have established a rough chronology of the rise of the various cultures of the Northwest, beginning, they think, with early man's exploitation of large mammals at the end of the Ice Age. This chronology points both to transformations taking place in the environment itself and to the amazing versatility of human enterprise revealed in the archaeological record.

Coastal region prehistory is divided roughly into four periods that span the last 12,000 years—the interval

These families are divided further into language groupings roughly equivalent to European groupings such as Germanic, Romantic or Slavic. As many as seven such groups, derived from two of the broader families, are present in Washington. These include Wakashan, Chimakuan and Salishan, three closely related groups of the northern coastal and interior regions; Sahaptin, Waiilatpuan and Chinookan, three distantly related groups of the Columbia River system; and Athabascan of the Na-Dene family, represented by the Kwalhioqua speakers of the Willapa Hills.

In order to overcome the broad disparity of native languages, Northwest Indians adopted a lingua franca of their own, prior to contact with whites. Chinook jargon, as it became known, was a simple vocabulary of terms used in commerce among tribes. It differed considerably from

following the retreat of the continental glaciers. In that time span, climate, sea level, vegetation and animal life-forms changed dramatically. The human presence, identified by the uncovering of numerous archaeological sites, always has capitalized on food and material near at hand. The record is one of progressive refinement in tools, diet, habitation sites and cultural practices.

The "Early Prehistoric" period, dating from about 12,000 years to about 6,000 B.P. (before present), was characterized by a dependence on land mammals, including bison and perhaps mastodon and caribou. Tool relics include fragments of crudely shaped basalt scrapers, choppers and abraders as well as simple bone tools. These inhabitants of the coastal lowlands traveled in small bands to sites where game animals were known to congregate—places like bogs and river terraces. The extent of their dependence on marine resources is unknown and coastal sites that they inhabited are probably now inundated by the sea.

The interval between approximately 6,000 and 3,000 years B.P. is known to coastal archaeologists as the "Middle Prehistoric" period. Although Washington State sites are not conclusive in their evidence of an economic orientation for the people of this time period, such sites show remarkable similarities to sites in coastal British Columbia. These sites reveal a growing dependence on marine resources, such as mussels and clams, while dependence on land mammals remains strong. The tool technology of these people incorporated new materials, such as slate and bone, in a growing diversity of projectile points. Pollen and other biological studies reveal that the coastal climate underwent a dramatic change during this period, which induced changes in the vegetation. The coastal forest, with its dense conifers, spread over the relatively open landscape of previous centuries and forever altered the economy of native peoples. The growth of forests focused their cultures in permanent sites and added to the store of materials at their disposal.

The third period recognized by archaeologists is called the "Early Maritime" period. Its dates are roughly 3,000 to 1,000 years B.P. It was during this period that coastal settlement living had been firmly adopted and salmon and other marine fishes became principal food sources. Familiarity with woodworking techniques is demonstrated by the presence of adze fragments at several sites. One site, at the mouth of the Hoko River,

Clockwise from left:
Bone barb, *possibly part of a fishing implement. Less than 500 years old.*
Projectile points *from Marmes Rockshelter, 6,000 to 10,000 years old, predate use of the bow and arrow.*
Cascade Phase *obsidian points, 5,000 to 6,000 years old, from Marmes Rockshelter. During the Cascade Phase, refinements in the techniques of forming and a regional trade in materials led to wider diversity of stone artifacts.* KARNA ORSEN PHOTOS

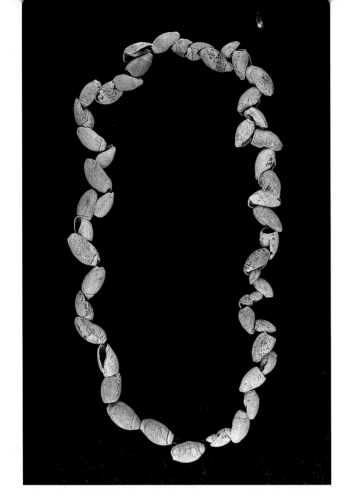

has been identified as a seasonal fishing camp. Here, evidence of a sophisticated fishery has been found, dating to between 2,200 and 2,700 years B.P. Weir fragments, bent hooks and a variety of fiber and wooden implements suggest that the use of plant materials had been mastered and that the use of stone had been refined to include carefully chipped stone blades used for filleting fish. Early Maritime sites often were perched on coastal headlands or at river mouths, an indication that their inhabitants lived in seasonal accord with marine resources. Such attentiveness, coupled with technological refinements of woodworking that allowed the construction of seaworthy canoes and large plank houses, gave rise to relatively large population centers and complex societies.

The 800-year period prior to the arrival of whites represented the culmination of a stone-flake technology based on wood, shell, antler, fiber and bone. Known as the "Prehistoric Northwest Coast Pattern," it was characterized by increased hunting of marine mammals and the development of highly stratified societies. Numerous sites have been excavated that date from this period. One site, Ozette near Cape Alava, yielded remains of entire households buried beneath tons of mud. Although artifacts removed and studied date back no further that 450 years, they present a vivid picture of the rich period when the many civilizations of the coastal Indians thrived.

People of the Interior

The sequence of cultural transformations unearthed at Eastern Washington archaeological sites suggests a general trend similar to that of the coast—generalists who gradually specialized as resources around them changed. Climate, land-use and vegetation patterns that differed between eastern and western Washington, however, have led to scientific study of more Eastern Washington sites, for three principal reasons. First, both the vegetation and landscape of the Columbia Plateau are more open; sites are more easily revealed. Second, with intensive grazing and farming during the settlement era, the landscape has been scrutinized in detail. Third, the massive dam and reservoir projects of the Columbia Basin have prompted (and funded) extensive "salvage" archaeological operations at cultural sites threatened by disturbance and flooding.

   With the benefit of more sites and greater detail in the data, a more complicated picture of human prehistory in Eastern Washington has emerged. Between about 11,000 and about 8,000 B.P., the landscape here was cold and barren. General warming did not bring forests and grasslands to the region until relatively late in the period. Archaeologists call this the "Windust Phase," after an important archaeological site along the Snake River. Human subsistence during this time is classified as "broad-spectrum foraging," which is the use of diverse resources and seasonal migration. Population was small, with scattered bands moving frequently between resource-rich sites in accordance with the migrations of birds and mammals and the ripening of plant seeds, roots and fruits. The most famous archaeological site of this period is the Marmes Rockshelter. At Marmes, a deep cleft in the basalt walls of the Palouse River canyon, signs of winter occupation were found, including remains of deer, elk, freshwater mussels and fish. Another Windust site, Lind Coulee, revealed signs of habitation during the spring, when bison calves were hunted and waterfowl nesting sites near Moses Lake were raided for eggs. Stone artifacts of this era consisted of short stone blades, crude cobble choppers and rough, lance-shaped projectile points.

   Between about 8,000 and 4,500 B.P., climatic conditions changed from relatively moist and cool to hotter and drier. Lower-elevation water sources dried up, plant and animal communities changed, and humans were forced into higher-elevation sites along tributary streams and into the forests that girdled the Columbia Basin. This interval is generally known to archaeologists as the "Cascade Phase." Like the earlier inhabitants of the

Manis site under excavation.
DR. CARL GUSTAFSON

"Tucannon" or "Frenchman Springs Phase." Grass invaded areas previously clothed in sage and conditions began to resemble those of today. Theorists suggest that temperature moderation also brought a rise in the level of rivers, perhaps with the broadening of floodplains. As plant communities became more productive, food and shelter were available to growing populations of animals. In turn, human population increased. Winter villages consisting of pithouses were established along terraces of the Columbia River and its tributary valleys, but were inhabited only briefly, probably during the harshest part of the year. Secondary residential areas also came into being, large base-camp–type villages in tributary canyons, where seasonal food resources were gathered and processed for transport to the winter villages where they were stored. Although it appears that large populations traveled a seasonal circuit among the camps, resource utilization appears to have occurred within a relative narrow band adjacent to the Columbia River. At most sites, rock artifacts are composed primarily of basalt found near the river. Projectile points typical of this age are crude, owing to the poor forming characteristics of basalt.

Aridity returned to the Columbia Basin about 2,500 years ago. Again, vegetation patterns and the whole productivity scheme of the region changed. Grassland areas were transformed into sage and widespread plant resources dwindled into isolated patches in moist localities. The interval between 2,500 and 250 B.P., is known as the "Harder" or "Cayuse Phase." For part of this time, population levels declined in the immediate vicinity of the Columbia and increased in the interior of the basin at places like Moses Lake, Quincy Basin and Saddle Mountain. After about 1,600 B.P., a subsistence pattern similar to that found at the time of contact with Europeans was in place—the repeated use of principal village sites during the winter and the specialization of groups who visited the same upland sites year after year to harvest concentrated resources like camas and huckleberries. Population increased and concentrated, but foraging territories became larger. Evidence of intensive salmon fishing is found at major rapids on the Columbia and at river junctions and rapids in the tributaries.

The final phase of prehistory recognized in Washington has been called the "Numípu Phase," based on the name the Nez Perce used for themselves. It is marked by

region, these people lived by foraging among a wide spectrum of plant and animal resources. Deer, elk, pronghorn antelope and mountain sheep were hunted, along with smaller animals including hares, bobcats, turtles, marmots and snakes. Salmon were also utilized, but only as one of many sources of food taken when opportunity presented itself. Grinding stones and stone grinding slabs, called *metates,* have been found, and probably were used for roots or meat. Smaller grinding stones also suggest that seeds were part of the diet.

From 4,500 to 2,500 B.P., the climate of the Columbia Basin moderated and clusters of trees appeared in the lower elevations. This time period is referred to as the

one event, which began the transformation of native cultures well in advance of the actual appearance of whites. It was the arrival of the horse, a cultural effect of the advance of Europeans into southern North America and a precursor of an impending whirlwind that would bring disease and change—biological and cultural chaos—to the Indian people throughout the New World.

The horse must indeed have been a wonder-inspiring addition to the Indian world. That it was so easily incorporated into the cultural ways of so many peoples of the West and that they developed mastery over equitation in such short time remains a fact astounding to historians and anthropologists. Arriving in the Columbia Basin sometime around 1730, by way of Shoshonean peoples of the Snake River plain, horses found an ecological niche among the rolling grasslands that rimmed the arid basins. Similarly, Indian people, whose seasonal wanderings between prime fishing locations and upland plateaus and river valleys rich in camas and berries required some degree of mobility, readily adopted the advantage that the beasts conferred.

The spread of horses into what is now Washington was constrained by the the presence of grasslands. The Yakima, Cayuse, Nez Perce, Okanogan and Spokane were the principal horse tribes at the time of contact with Europeans. The impact of a wider use of horses was profound, both in terms of the extension of pre-equine culture patterns and the adoption of new ones. For tribes that dominated the great fisheries, it enabled transport of massive quantities of salmon (in dried and baled form) to people at remote localities. The ecological impact of grazing horses is thought to have included competition with native deer and elk, which displaced or depressed wildlife availability. This in turn required extended forays to previously remote regions for hunting. Thus, the new mobility not only was facilitated by the horse, but perhaps was necessary because of it. Territories expanded and frequently overlapped, forcing the melding of cultures among horse Indians. Additionally, incursions of horse-borne enemies, such as the "Snakes" (actually Paiutes), forced adjustments in territory.

The River Harvest

If any ecological theme unites all the Indians of what is now Washington, it would be the subsistence pattern based upon salmon. Coastal and interior rivers

surged with the annual silver tides of fish, bringing nutrients to the people and conferring material advantage upon those who settled at places where the fish were most easily taken. The relatively intensive activity required to catch, process and store large quantities of food—particularly when availability is as brief as that of salmon—required a high degree of social organization and lent itself to permanent village life. At places like Kettle Falls, the cataracts of the Klickitat, Celilo Falls, Priest Rapids and many other sites where water boiled in deep pools beneath rushing cascades, permanent fishing villages were established and human population swelled when the salmon were in the river.

The salmon penetrated far up the Columbia River system and deep into the mountainous heartland of the

Dr. Carl Gustafson and mastodon jaws during excavation of Manis site, 1979. DELBERT GILBOW

Cascades, Okanogan Highlands and western ranges of the Rockies, linking the Plains-influenced tribes of eastern Washington with the tidewater Indians of Puget Sound in the circle of seasons and the cycles of survival. Throughout the archaeological record on both sides of the Cascade Mountains, the progression of subsistence patterns reflects increased dependency upon salmon as the principal food source for the whole year. Early, generalized utilization of large mammals and a variety of plants was supplemented by the seasonal use of fresh fish. Over the millenia, methods of drying, storing and trading allowed year-round use of the protein-rich river harvest.

Various studies have been conducted to determine the extent of Indian exploitation of salmon prior to the coming of whites. The first observations were made by Lewis and Clark, who passed the great salmon fishery at Celilo Falls in the fall, while the preparation of dried salmon was in full swing. William Clark noted that "I counted 107 stacks of dried pounded fish in different places on those rocks which must have contained 10,000 lb of neet fish" [*sic*]. In 1846, Canadian artist Paul Kane visited Kettle Falls, writing that "the chief told me that he had taken as many as 1700 salmon, weighing an average of 30 lbs. each, in the course of one day." Certainly, by this time the aboriginal fishery was at its high point. Later estimates suggest that the total catch of salmon throughout the Columbia Basin, based on the nutritional requirements of the Indians and weighted variously by the relative importance of salmon within each tribe, may have exceeded 41 million pounds per year, or 4.5 to 6.3

million fish. But this massive quantity amounts to only about half of what fisheries biologists have calculated as the total run size for Columbia River salmon before the arrival of whites. In terms of the impact of Native American fisheries on the salmon resource, biologists suggest that the broad dispersion of fisheries throughout the Columbia system was, in fact, highly conducive to the conservation of individual fish runs.

If dispersion of the fisheries over the vast network of waterways formed a natural mechanism to balance the Indians' take of fish, the recognition of a higher bond among humans and all living things, including salmon, established cultural limits. The first-salmon ceremony recognized this connection and established a set of constraints on human behavior designed to ensure that salmon remained plentiful. It was, like similar "first fruits" ceremonies with other resources such as roots and berries, a way of expressing gratitude to those specific entities of the cosmos that nurtured the human body and community. Typical of a pattern found throughout much of salmon country, the season's first fish symbolized the return of the First Fish, the leader or messenger from the salmon people. Erna Gunther, a pioneer anthropologist who studied the first-salmon ceremony extensively in the 1920s, wrote, "the pattern for the salmon ceremony seems to be based on a reverential attitude toward the fish and a desire to treat it in such a manner that it will come in great numbers." At Wishram, on the Washington side of the Columbia near Celilo Falls, she reported that upon catching the first salmon of the spring migrations, "the people would stop fishing until a ceremony could be organized. The fisherman would take the fish to the shaman who would cut it lengthwise and remove the backbone and head in one piece. The fish is baked in a depression in the ground, which is lined with choke-cherry leaves and covered with mats. Everyone is invited and gets some fish. They pray at the feast. The bones are not returned to the river."

Following the ceremony, fishing would begin in earnest, and would proceed until the last of the fish straggled to the cascades. Such a ceremony is evidence that these people regarded the world and their place in it as fluid and alive. They also recognized that balance for people hinged on the balance of a complete network of living things.

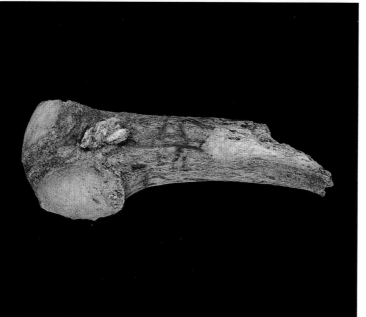

Above: Formed cobble, possibly a net weight or a club head.

Above left: Grinding pestles, Marmes site, less than 4,000 to 5,000 years old.

Left: A pointed bone fragment lodged in the rib of a mastodon suggests that early man hunted the hairy elephants as ice receded from the Puget Lowlands about 12,000 years ago. From the Manis site near Sequim. KARNA ORSEN PHOTOS

CHAPTER FOUR

EXPLORATION

Above: *Sea otter* (Enhydra lutris) *cracking clam on rock.*
TOM & PAT LEESON
Right: *Near The Dalles.* CHRISTIAN HEEB

By Sea

The appearance of Europeans on the Northwest Coast began as a competition between England and Spain for world sea dominance. It grew to a frenzy over commercial opportunity presented in the trade of furs—sea otters on the coast and beaver inland. It subsided when a new power—the United States—appeared and absorbed the Northwest as it had much of the rest of North America. Over a period of about 75 years, the land that is now Washington State was, in minute scale, the scene of shifts of world power that enveloped greater regions with far more visible effects. The only signs we have today of the various waves of exploration are the names, a scattering of Spanish among a preponderance of English: the occasional "Haro" or "Eliza" mingled with the "Rainiers," the "Elds" and the "Hoods."

There is agreement that Sir Francis Drake visited the west coast of North America during his globe-circling voyage of 1579. His own claims placed his northward progress along our coast to Latitude 48, or just south of Cape Alava. Nineteenth-century scholars felt that Latitude 43 was more probable; nevertheless, the perception of his visit to the region had historic significance. Either way, English claims for what Drake called "New Albion" (Albion was a Roman name for the British Isles) prompted the rival Spanish to reinforce their own claims to the land thought to contain passage to the Orient—the mythical Northwest Passage.

Michael Lok's story of a northwest passage became widely known throughout the seafaring world sometime around 1596, following a remarkable encounter Lok had in Venice with an aging "Pilot of Shippes" by the name of Juan de Fuca. The pilot, according to the story, had served the Spanish in the New World between 1588 and 1594.

De Fuca's second voyage resulted in the discovery of a "broad Inlet of Sea, betweene 47. and 48. degrees of Latitude…at the entrance of this said Strait, there is on the North-west coast thereof, a great Hedland or Iland, with an exceeding high Pinacle, or spired Rocke, like a piller thereupon." The land the inlet penetrated, according to de Fuca, was rich in gold, silver and pearls and was peopled by inhabitants who dressed in the skins of beasts. The voyage to the Atlantic was made and retraced, with the pilot returning to Mexico, where he received a warm welcome from the viceroy and the promise of riches from the King of Spain himself, as a reward for his discovery.

De Fuca travelled to Spain, but received no riches. Disgruntled, he washed his hands of the Spanish and sought to share his information with England. His entreaties denied, de Fuca returned to his Greek homeland, and according to Lok, died around 1602. Partly because Lok was a promoter of expeditions to the Northwest Passage, and partly because the story had such magnetic appeal, de Fuca's fable galvanized the imagination and hope of every navigator with designs on the Northwest Coast.

Spain's presence in the Northwest grew, through modest excursions northward from Mexico. In 1774, Juan Perez commanded a voyage of the *Santiago* to about Latitude 55 (just north of the Queen Charlotte Islands) and erected several crosses of possession, but made no attempt to settle any of the coastal lands he claimed. Traveling south, Perez observed a glistening peak at Latitude 48° 10′, which he named El Cerro Nevada de Santa Rosalia (the snowy hill of St. Rosalia). According to historian Edmund S. Meany, it was the first European-named landscape feature of what was to become the State of Washington. At a later date, the mountain became known as "Olympus."

The *Santiago* returned in 1775, under the command of Bruno Heceta. Accompanying was the schooner *Sono-*

John Sykes

ra, under the command of Juan Francisco Bodega y Quadra. After a combined party succeeded in planting the cross of possession on what is now Point Grenville, a crew of six men from the *Sonora* went ashore for firewood and water. The party was surprised by Indians and murdered. Upon their departure, the Spanish named a small island in the vicinity, "Isla de Dolores"—island of the sorrows. Today, the island bears the name "Destruction Island."

Voyages of the English

The English were not far behind. In 1775, Parliament had approved a £20,000 reward for the first commander of a British merchantman to discover a passage between the Atlantic and Pacific north of Latitude 52. The offer was extended to explorer Capt. James Cook and instructions for his third Pacific voyage included orders to explore "such rivers or inlets as may appear to be of considerable extent and pointing towards Hudson's or Baffin's Bays." Care was to be taken not to offend any competing European power; nevertheless, establishing claims to any previously unclaimed land was to be a priority.

Vancouver's exploration of Puget Sound relied on precise astronomical data gathered from instruments placed on the shore. Here, his observatory at a site in present-day Discovery Bay, Strait of Juan de Fuca.

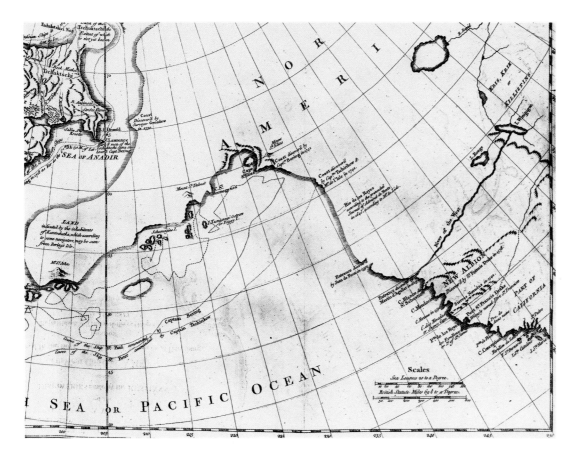

The Northwest Coast defied geographic knowledge by Europeans late in the 18th century. This map, attributed to Jeffreys, dates from 1764.
COURTESY OREGON HISTORICAL SOCIETY, NUMBER 23938

Cook's voyage to the Northwest Coast brought him in 1778 to what is now Washington. Cook approached the coast during March, in weather so threatening that twice he retreated offshore rather than risk being blown onto the rocky headlands. One of his approaches brought him near "the pretended Strait of Juan de Fuca," where he left the name "Flattery" inscribed on his chart to mark a prominent headland. His work, however, was to the north, and to that work he sped. His untimely death in the Hawaiian Islands, less than a year later, prevented him from knowing that his failure to recognize the fabled strait at Cape Flattery was a major blunder in his otherwise spectacular career.

It was Cook's discovery of the value the Chinese placed on sea otter pelts that led entrepreneurs of various maritime nations to the Northwest Coast. Cook's crew acquired a few skins at Nootka, the captain apparently

recognizing the animal from descriptions of earlier Russian explorers. According to historian Hubert Howe Bancroft, the men had no idea of the skins' value—some were fashioned into bedclothes and many were damaged or spoiled. Nevertheless, the skins fetched nearly $10,000 in Macao, an island off the Chinese mainland. Cook's sailors clamored to return to the Northwest Coast to engage in the otter-skin trade. Although they did not, the word quickly spread and within a few years' time, ships were being outfitted for the lucrative trade. Merchant vessels of many flags soon made calls at coastal points and embayments where Indians proffered otter skins in exchange for sheets of copper and other highly prized European goods.

The voyage of Capt. George Vancouver to the Northwest Coast in 1792 grew out of matters left somewhat unresolved by Cook's visit. One item on Vancouver's agenda was diplomatic—he carried instructions to represent England in the settlement of the "Nootka Incident," which had brought Spain and England to the brink of war following a series of petty misunderstandings in which English commercial and strategic interests had run head-on into those of Spain. The capture of English vessels and their crews by the Spanish and an inflammatory and overstated memorial to Parliament by John Meares had initiated a precarious seesaw of tenuous dominance over the outpost at Friendly Cove on Nootka Sound. Great Britain geared up for war. By the time Vancouver met with Bodega y Quadra, his Iberian counterpart, events had shifted and instructions to both negotiators proved irrelevant to a speedy resolution. Amicably admitting the futility of their encounter as diplomats, the two leaders nevertheless exchanged charts of the region, and, in honor of their work together, gave the name "Vancouver and Bodega y Quadra's Island" to the great land body now known by an abbreviated name, Vancouver Island.

Exploration of the coast proved the true fruit of the Vancouver voyage. Well prepared to carry on the work of the Great Navigator, Vancouver had served on Cook' second and third journeys and was now in command of the *Discovery,* newly commissioned but named after one of Cook's ships. Carrying the most advanced chronometers of the day (they were hopelessly unreliable), he and his officers labored meticulously to accurately chart each feature of the coast. Crossing the Pacific from the Hawaiian Islands, the *Discovery,* in consort with the armed tender *Chatham,* approached the continent at Cape Mendocino.

The ships moved northward along the continental shore, taking sightings on prominent headlands and other shore features. They missed the Columbia River mouth, although naturalist Archibald Menzies thought he detected signs of the great stream. Off what is now the Washington coast, they met Robert Gray, an American merchant busily gathering furs for the China trade. Gray informed them of his successful penetration of the Strait of Juan de Fuca and, as they parted, he watched the British with suspicion, fearing that their true mission was that of gathering furs.

On April 29, 1792, Vancouver entered the Strait. On May 2, the ships anchored at what is now Discovery Bay, where Vancouver repaired the ships, aired the damp powder, brewed spruce beer to stave off scurvy, and established a temporary observatory for making celestial sightings to establish precise position. From Discovery Bay, he dispatched a longboat that crept along the beach to the southernmost point of Hood Canal. On May 18, the ships entered what Vancouver called "Admiralty Inlet," the passage that led southward from the eastern end of the Strait of Juan de Fuca. It was the first time that the creaking wooden ships of white men had entered what is now Puget Sound. Where the larger ships themselves did not explore, the boats under sail and oar did. A party commanded by Lt. Peter Puget probed the central basin and southern extremities of the sound. Puget's circuit through the south sound included passage into Carr and Case inlets, west of Hartstene and Squaxin islands and into Totten, Eld and Budd inlets, up through Nisqually Reach, the (Tacoma) Narrows, Colvos Passage (west of Vashon Island) and back to *Discovery*'s anchorage off Bainbridge Island.

In all, the *Discovery* made 18 anchorages in Puget Sound and the Strait of Juan de Fuca and left names on dozens of landmark features including Mt. Rainier, Mt. Baker, and many waterways, bays, channels, points and islands. Continuing out of the inland sea according to the method of their survey, they cruised north through Rosario Strait. On June 11, the ships anchored at Birch Bay, their last anchorage in Washington waters. Between the 11th and the 24th, boat expeditions out from the ships surveyed waters to the north and on June 23, the ships departed northward to overtake their boats and move on for Nootka. Convinced that the Northwest Passage itself was not at hand, Vancouver nevertheless placed a great network of waterways on the map and a host of names upon the land.

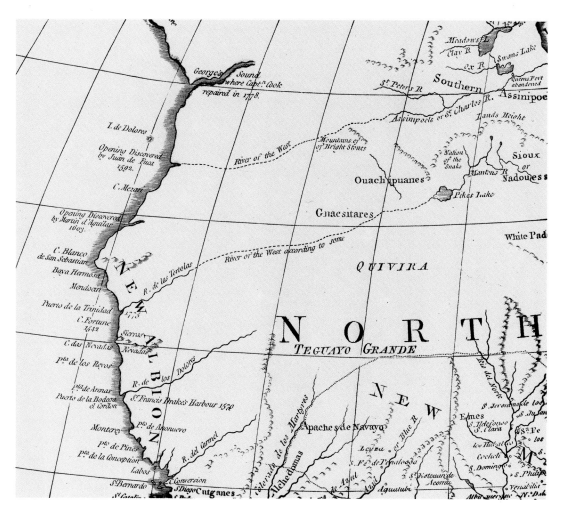

Following his meeting with Vancouver, Capt. Gray had turned south and paid watchful attention to two suspected yet undiscovered features of the coast. One was the great estuary approximately at Latitude 47, which he entered and named Bulfinch Harbor, after one of his financial backers. It was later renamed Grays Harbor in honor of its discoverer. The other, a great river whose broad entrance was guarded by a tempest of currents and breakers, had resisted his efforts to enter on several earlier attempts. On May 11, guided by a small boat sounding a route among the shoals, the *Columbia Rediviva* entered the fabled river and established what was to be an author-

Cook's visit, along with those of the Spanish, put some names on this sparsely illustrated map of the Northwest of 1786, attributed to Sagar. De Fuca's "opening," and various "Rivers of the West" remained ambiguous—did they exist on the face of the land or in the minds of the fanciful? COURTESY OREGON HISTORICAL SOCIETY, NUMBER 27392

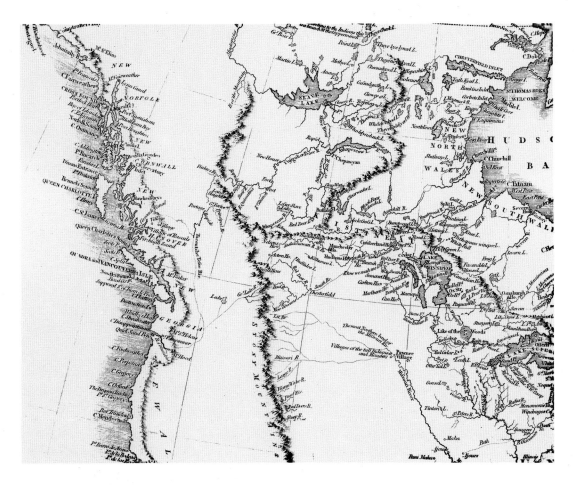

Above: *Vancouver's 1792 charting of the Strait of Juan de Fuca and Lewis and Clark's 1805-1806 journey along the Columbia established the veracity of some rumored geographic features. The land's dual points of entry shaped the unfolding events that would follow. 1806 map, attributed to John Carey, reveals increasing knowledge.* COURTESY OREGON HISTORICAL SOCIETY, NUMBER 27393.

Facing page: *Samuel Walker's 1825 map fills in more intermountain regions of the Northwest.* COURTESY OREGON HISTORICAL SOCIETY, NUMBER 27390

itative American claim to a piece of the Northwest Coast. Gray patriotically added American names to the charts: Cape Hancock, the point to the north; Cape Adams, the point to the south; and Columbia, after his ship, the magnificent waterway itself. To the swirl of nations with growing interests and claims in the Northwest, the young nation on North America's Atlantic shore was conjoined.

By Land

The headlong rush that attended the search for the Northwest Passage had quieted some by the end of the 18th century. Yet, where no arm of sea had been discovered there persisted reports of a passage facilitated by way of a great river. Indeed, the lower reaches of the Columbia were known and had been charted. Where it rose out of the mountains was not known, and what advantage it would confer was still subject to speculation.

While sea-otter furs proved the commercial resource that drew merchants to the coast, it was the beaver that drew fur traders overland. In 1670, the Hudson's Bay Company was granted commercial rights to most of British North America. In 1787, the Northwest Company was formed, operating from Montreal through the vast network of lakes and portages that stretched westward to the Rockies. Both companies established a commercial frontier of trading posts and trade routes heavily reliant on Indians who hunted, clerks who operated the posts and dealt in the currency of lush pelage, voyageurs who moved the goods through the maze of northern waterways and magnificent bureaucracies, which established policies and maintained tight fiscal control over the companies' empires. Although exploration itself was a necessary component of the fur trade, it remained an accessory to commercial ventures rather than an end in itself.

It was an American overland expedition, led by Meriwether Lewis and William Clark, that connected the fledgling United States to the then-remote Pacific shore. In his instructions to Capt. Lewis, President Thomas Jefferson outlined an ambitious set of tasks, requiring skills in disciplines as varied as ethnology, meteorology, botany and geology—a breadth of interests not unlike his own.

Jefferson's instructions to Meriwether Lewis (who had previously served as his personal secretary) included the following broad objective: "The object of your mission is to explore the Missouri river, & such principal stream of it, as, by it's [sic] course & communication with the water of the Pacific Ocean may offer the most direct & practicable water communication across this continent, for the purposes of commerce." The expedition had two missions, one scientific (designed not to raise the ire of foreign powers sensing incipient competition), the other commercial—with aims toward understanding the vast region west of the Mississippi. Known as Louisiana, these lands had passed from Spain to France in 1800 and from France to the United States in 1803. In seeking an appropriation from the ever-practical Congress, Jefferson emphasized the commercial aspect of the expedition; exploration for the sake of science was, as yet, not within the nation's means.

Lt. William Clark was chosen as Lewis' co-commander and promoted to the rank of captain. The expedition left St. Louis in the fall of 1804, wintered with the Mandans and resumed the westward journey up the Missouri in the spring of 1805. Entering the Rockies, the party spent torturous months probing the maze of drainages and divides, emerging finally over Lolo Pass and descending the Clearwater River. On October 10, 1805, they reached the confluence of the Clearwater and Snake rivers, marking the first overland advance of whites into what would become Washington Territory within 50 years and the 33rd state of the union within 85 years. Lewis and Clark moved quickly over the Columbia Plain and through the Columbia Gorge, arriving at the Pacific in a grim, drizzly November.

During their stay at the mouth of the Columbia, members of the expedition explored the lowland between what is now Ilwaco and the Long Beach Peninsula and engaged in lively trade with Indians residing on both sides of the river. Lewis wrote, "Although we have not fared sumptuously the past winter and spring at Fort Clatsop, we have lived quite as comfortably as we had any reason to expect…" It had been Lewis' hope that they would meet a trading vessel while at the river's mouth, but none appeared. Before they departed for the return trek, they prepared a roster of the expedition's membership with a brief description of their task and left it with the Indians, to be given to a trading vessel. At 1 p.m., Sunday March 23, 1806, the party abandoned their winter encampment and began their return trek to St. Louis, where they arrived to great fanfare at noon, on the 23rd of September.

According to historian William H. Goetzmann, the primary accomplishment of the Lewis and Clark expedition was that it put to rest the principal compelling objective that had driven explorers for centuries in their Northwest quests—a direct water link to the riches of the Orient. The turning point of this political and economic geography was the realization of the vastness of the North American west and its abundance of riches. At last, the eyes of the explorers turned toward the land itself and away from the chimerical mists of the exotic faraway. Indeed, as the legacy of oceanic rivalry subsided, a new one quickened. Between the empire of Great Britain, represented by the commercial interests of the Hudson's Bay and the Northwest companies, and the republic of the United States, represented by a few precarious business enterprises, some Protestant missionaries and a trickle of immigrants, a political tug-of-war was brewing. What we now call Washington was to be a large part of the prize.

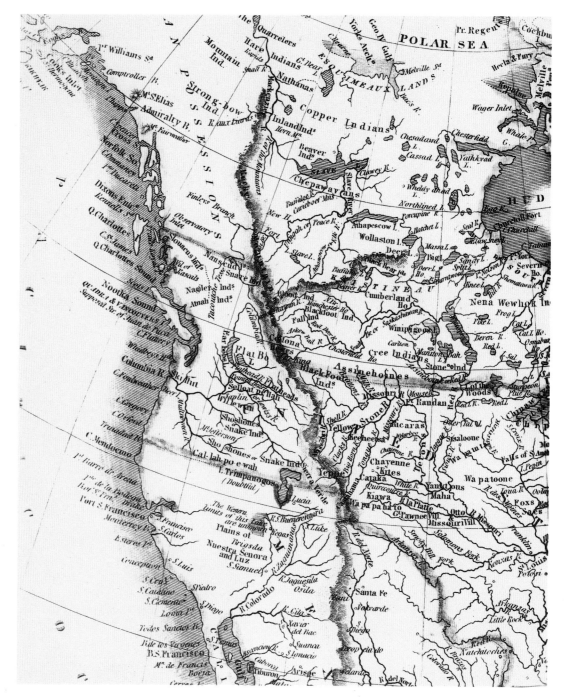

A Network of Fur Companies

Gradually, as the influence of the fur companies spread, their network of posts expanded. In 1807, David Thompson, an impeccably trained surveyor as well as an able Hudson's Bay Company man, travelled up the Saskatchewan River, crossed the continental divide at Howse Pass and encountered a large river flowing northwest. Although his great hope was that he would find the Columbia that earlier Canadian explorers had missed, he failed to recognize the great river when he did. Here, deep in the heart of the Canadian Rockies, the Columbia wanders far to the north before doubling south and eventually breaching the continental ranges. Moving instead to the southeast, Thompson established a string of company posts in the Kootenay, Kalispell, Pend Oreille and Spokane regions, extending the territorial grasp of the Northwest Company southward. In 1811, after establishing Spokane House, he realized that he had at last found the main stem of the Columbia. Upon reaching the mouth of the Snake River, he erected a pole and attached a paper claiming the land for Great Britain and announcing his intention to establish a post at that location. Proceeding downstream, he reached the mouth of the Great River of the West on July 14 only to find at that site the upstart Pacific Fur Company of the American John Jacob Astor. In what would have been a rapid conquest of the southern Rocky Mountain fur districts and the trading artery that was the Columbia River, the Canadian had been beaten by a hair's breadth. Domination over the Columbia country would not be easy.

New York investor John Jacob Astor's enterprise represented Yankee commercial interest in the fur bounty of the Far West. In addition, it fostered the opening of another major overland corridor to the Northwest, for the Astor party had two vanguards, one by sea (which had established the post at "Astoria") and another by land, which reached the outpost in tattered form in February 1812. Intent on using the Lewis and Clark route over Lolo Pass, the overlanders swerved off-route to avoid hostile Blackfoot Indians and were lucky to find any route whatsoever into the Columbia River valley. On an eastward journey to report on the Astorians' progress, however, Robert Stuart and party found their way through South Pass, into the Platte River Valley and on to St. Louis. With this, the Oregon Trail had been discovered. In the race between David Thompson and the Americans, two great

fur-trade routes had been discovered that converged on the mouth of the Columbia—the Montreal-Saskatchewan River-Athabasca Pass route to the north and the St. Louis-Platte River-South Pass route of the south. Poised for head-to-head competition for the new region were two powerful national destinies; ahead were decades of deadlock over the final disposition of territorial sovereignty.

Pressing events on the international front shaped the first round of competition: The War of 1812 placed England and the United States at military odds. Although the Astorians had built a cozy if struggling commercial empire around them, the arrival of a troop of vaguely belligerent Northwesterners at Astoria and news of the imminent appearance of the warship HMS *Raccoon,* with orders to bombard the Americans' outpost and take the furs stored there as spoils of war, prompted the Astor

company to hastily sell all of its interests at what Astor later estimated to be about 33 cents on the dollar.

Disgraced in the end, the Astor venture nevertheless asserted the American place at the mouth of the Columbia. And through its agency, the empire in the making had linked the point where Gray had established the American maritime presence in the South Pass corridor, through which a flood of immigrants would eventually promote a conquest that would displace the British. As the era of exploration ended the question of sovereignty remained far from resolved. The apocryphal charts of a Northwest Passage had been replaced by more accurate ones: those of Vancouver, Lewis and Clark, and Thompson. History had changed the purpose of the Northwest Passage, from one envisioned to bypass the western wilderness to one that would open it.

Above: Fort Astoria, the Yankee outpost where Americans made a brief bid for the beaver-fur trade. COURTESY EASTERN WASHINGTON HISTORICAL SOCIETY

Facing page: Beaver (Castor canadensis). TOM & PAT LEESON

CHAPTER FIVE

THE TAMING

Above: *Snowberry checkerspot butterfly on a bistort flower.* TOM & PAT LEESON
Right: *"Early Morning View of Tongue Point." Circa 1883, by Cleveland Rockwell.*
COURTESY COLUMBIA MARITIME MUSEUM, ASTORIA
#67.104A

If any period of Washington history can be considered pivotal in terms of the pace and overall shape of settlement patterns, it would be that between 1846, when Joint Occupancy with Great Britain was finally resolved, and 1859, when the terms of the Stevens treaties with the Indians were ratified by Congress.

Although 18th-century explorers had failed to find a shortcut to the Orient when they charted the Northwest's coastal waters, the twin revelations of an extensive inland sea, Puget Sound, and the lower reaches of the River of the West, the Columbia, were great consolations.

The geography of settlement in what became Washington followed a pattern imposed by the two waterways. Each was a corridor into the new land, the Strait of Juan de Fuca and the lower Columbia affording a seaward opening and the Columbia, by way of its tributaries, opening landward routes.

United States Versus Great Britain

With the negotiation of the Treaty of Ghent, ending the War of 1812 between the United States and Great Britain, the U.S. and England each maintained a claim to the region between the Columbia River and the 49th Parallel. This arrangement was formalized in 1818 as a compromise and was extended in 1827 under terms known as the Joint Occupancy. The Americans were not nearly so successful as the English in retaining a commercial presence in the Northwest—the Northwest Fur Company of John Jacob Astor had failed in its permanent settlement at Astoria, while the Hudson's Bay Company had established an enduring string of posts along the Columbia. With the establishment of Fort Vancouver in 1825, the British were firmly entrenched at the principal crossroads of the Northwest. In 1833, Nisqually House was established to the north to help secure the safety of company traders working in the Puget Sound region.

Nisqually became the functioning administrative center for all of Puget Sound. Although the company's principal business was the fur trade, expansion into agricultural production was natural, given ready markets in Alaska for beef and butter, and in England for hides. In 1839, the Puget Sound Agricultural Company formed. In the lowland prairies surrounding the post, more than a thousand cattle were grazed, watched by a handful of retired Hudson's Bay Company employees, who, as settlers, would be used to support England's claim to the disputed territory. By the time the boundary dispute was settled, the Hudson's Bay Company's Columbia Division east of the Cascades was in jeopardy, having no agricultural enterprises to replace the weakening fur market.

It was not until 1846 that the question of territorial sovereignty was resolved in favor of the United States. Under Joint Occupancy, increasing numbers of Americans had enjoyed the benefits of the economy the British had established. Economic conditions of the Mississippi Valley following the Panic of 1837 had forced many who had wandered that far to look farther to the west. Most early settlers came from agrarian backgrounds, and the abundance of good farmland promised great opportunity. By 1843, the Great Migration was in full swing, most travelers following the overland routes. Political philosophies of the emigrants contrasted sharply with those of the Hudson's Bay Company, although the pioneers held capable administrators like John McLoughlin and William Fraser Tolmie in high esteem. The question of the Northwest's ultimate political disposition for most settlers hinged more on aspirations of nationalism than on the day-to-day events on the frontier.

A foggy October morning on a Methow Valley farm. JEFF GNASS

Prior to the settlement of the international boundary dispute, the ultimate status of lands to the north of the Columbia River was uncertain. When the border was fixed along the 49th Parallel, American settlers moved into the Cowlitz River Valley and into the Puget Sound Basin itself. The earliest settlers reached present-day Thurston County in 1845. Larger numbers spilled into Tumwater and Olympia in 1846.

A new force began to emerge in the Columbia River country even while fur trapping had remained lucrative, a force that also would affect Washington Territory. Based largely on accounts that had been carried east by fur trappers, interest in the spiritual well-being of the Indians had prompted several Protestant groups to develop mission programs for the West. Methodists had been the first to establish missions, with Jason Lee organizing a network of Methodist outposts in the Willamette Valley and at The Dalles as early as the 1830s. In 1834, the American Board of Commissioners for Foreign Missions, which represented Congregationalist, Presbyterian and Dutch Reformed

churches, sent Dr. Marcus Whitman west to assess the potential for mission work among Northwest Indians. In 1836, Whitman, his wife Narcissa, and a party of others arrived at Fort Vancouver after having passed through the rich prairie lands of Walla Walla country, where they desired to return and to work among the Cayuse.

As fervent in opposing Catholicism as in opposing the tribes' traditional religions, the Protestants had been disturbed by the influence of Catholic missionaries working among the fur traders. The Catholics had a ready congregation among the trappers and their mixed-blood families because most of the fur hunters were of French-Canadian descent. Less high-handed in cultural bias, unencumbered with the Protestants' preoccupation with agriculture, and free of the family burdens of the Protestants, the Fathers worked the far-flung circuits of remote villages and established missions in the Bitterroot and Coeur d'Alene country. Eventually, the Roman Catholics expanded into much of the Columbia River valley, teaching among the Spokanes, Kalispells, Yakimas, Nez Perces and others.

While the Catholics worked in relative harmony, frustration marked both the Lee and Whitman Protestant missionary ventures. The Indians showed little interest in spiritual change, although some seemed to accept agricultural ways. Whitman especially became vexed because his dual purpose of converting Indian people to Christianity and to agrarian ways was being subverted by the Indians' preference for the secular aspects of his teachings (especially as they became better traders of produce as increasing numbers of Oregon-bound settlers arrived). The role of the mission itself was called into question as it became more of a resupply station for the material needs of advancing pioneers than the spiritual needs of the natives. As the flood of wagons quickened, so too the Indians became increasingly suspicious of Whitman's motives. Disease accompanied the settlers, devastating the Indian populations. Because Whitman treated the diseases, he was linked, in the minds of the Indians, to their spread. In 1847, in a martyrdom that is a historic watershed in Northwest history, the Whitmans' mission ended. With it, the mission era of eastern Washington ended, ushering in the military era—the dramatic climax of the series of cultural clashes and crossed purposes.

At the time of the Whitman massacre, federal presence in the Northwest had been non-existent. Although the treaty provisions of 1846 gave the United States the

land, whatever order Americans imposed over the territory was strictly home-grown. A provisional government was established that created some legal framework for such need as processing land claims and balancing the interests of the Americans and the remaining Hudson's Bay Company employees. The United States government, however, was temporarily indisposed by war with Mexico, conquest in California and wracking debate over slavery. Only when shocked by the hand-carried news of the Whitman massacre did Congress hasten to settle its obligation in Oregon country by establishing the Oregon Territory in 1847.

Response to the Whitman killings fell to local militia, which were poorly organized, poorly disciplined, and frequently motivated by immediate blood satisfaction. With the creation of Oregon Territory, regular Army forces were brought to the scene gradually. Their task, it turned out, would be as much to protect Indians from territorial militiamen as to protect the growing settlements from the swelling wrath of the native people.

The creation of Oregon Territory in 1848 firmly established administrative and political control over the region. Territorial politics were fast and furious, fueled by passion for the newly realized patrimony and a keen sense of self-interest. Although the political agenda for the Northwest centered on the practical matters of the homefront, debates growing on the national scene moved westward with the pioneers. The issue of slavery became as divisive here as in the rest of the Union. Its influence was especially profound because of the peculiar mix of the settlers' geographic origins and outlooks toward the prevention of slavery-related troubles. Other developments outside the region also profoundly influenced the settlers' fortunes. The California gold strikes promised ready markets for agricultural goods, timber and oysters. Although many settlers abruptly left for the gold fields, enough returned with handsome earnings that local economies felt direct benefit. Northwest commerce ensured that the empire a-building would be connected to the larger world.

The decade of the 1850s was not so much one of expansion as one of explosion. From an 1849 census of 9,000 white residents the territorial population swelled to 64,000 in 1860. For Washington, the 1850s was the decade that a distinct geopolitical identity was carved out of what had been known as Oregon.

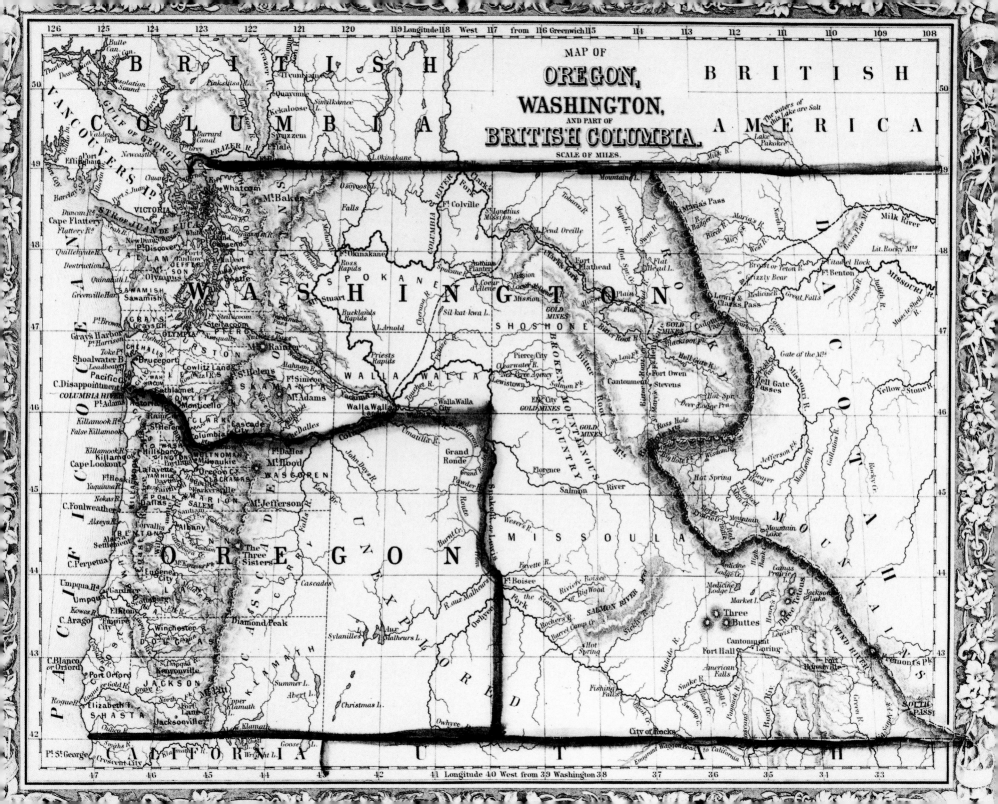

MAP OF
OREGON,
WASHINGTON,
AND PART OF
BRITISH COLUMBIA.
SCALE OF MILES.

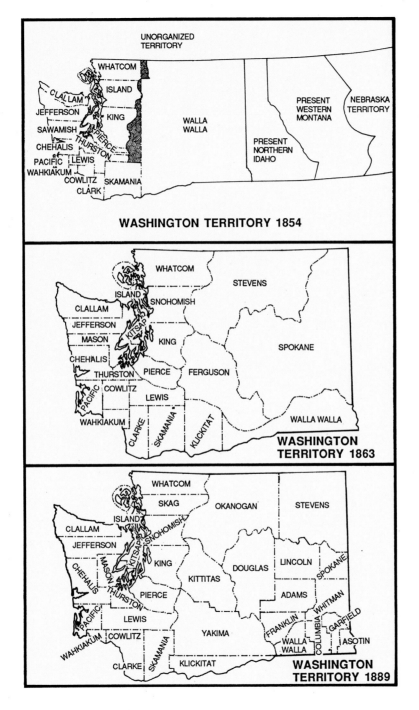

The evolution of Washington counties through the territorial period.
LAUREL BLACK

Creating Washington Territory

Agitation for organization of a territory between the Columbia River and the 49th Parallel grew out of what was perceived as Oregon territorial officials' indifference in matters pertaining to the northern districts. Laws could not be enforced because the territorial sheriff was not required to cross the Columbia. The territorial legislature seemed preoccupied with a tug-of-war for the capital between Oregon City and Salem. Northern representatives supported Oregon City and, although bolstered by the governor and the courts, protested in futility as a majority of the legislature repaired to Salem and commenced the 1851 legislative session. The disaffection resulted in the October 25, 1852, Monticello Convention, held near the mouth of the Cowlitz River. At the convention, a memorial to Congress was drafted for the creation of the Territory of Columbia. The proposed territory extended north and west of the Columbia River, south of the 49th Parallel and east of the Pacific.

The Oregon territorial legislature also favored the division, memorializing Congress themselves a week later. Former governor Joseph Lane, by 1852 the territorial delegate to Congress, argued before Congress in support of the arrangement. In a hastily conceived gesture of fervent patriotism, Columbia Territory became Washington Territory when Sen. Richard H. Stanton of Kentucky suggested the name change during Senate debate. Lane agreed and on March 2, 1853 the bill passed the Senate. President Millard Fillmore signed it two days before his term ended. Somewhere in the process, the eastern boundary had been extended to the summit of the Rocky Mountains, effectively doubling the territory in size. The vast tract that is now western Montana, northern Idaho and all of Washington State had been removed from Oregon Territory and bestowed a political and cultural life of its own.

Pioneer Phoebe Judson wrote in her diary: "When we left home the point of our destination was Puget Sound, 'Oregon.' We started the first day of March, and later in the same month Washington was created, by severing from Oregon all the country north of the Columbia. There was a slight sense of disappointment at the change of name, for the word 'Oregon' had grown very dear to me as the name of the country wherein lay my 'ideal home.' But 'a rose by any other name would smell as sweet,' and I soon grew reconciled to the change. Washington is a name that is suggestive of all that is noble, grand and good."

Although creation of Washington Territory meant political unification, distinct cultural differences remained among the settlers because of the territory's sharp geographic divisions. The decades just before and after the establishment of Washington Territory were characterized by power plays staged around themes of conflicting enterprise—old duels such as American interests versus British; Protestant versus Catholic; sacred versus secular and, finally, territorial versus federal. Roots of other differences reached well into the past. Communities on Puget Sound had been formed by New Englanders, familiar in commerce and shipping, at home with the benefits of the maritime environment. The Chehalis and Cowlitz valleys and the Vancouver region bore the cultural influences of the old Oregon Territory—agrarian pioneers carried through America's heartland in the urge westward.

East of the mountains, settlement was predominantly accomplished by the overland settler. At Fort Hall, the American emigrants continued to Fort Boise, from there into Columbia country, into the Walla Walla and around the sweeping bend through Wallula along the scabland basalt terraces of the mighty river. Some liked the relatively moist valley soils of the Walla Walla enough to stay, rather than proceed west across the Cascades into the Willamette Valley.

The creation of Washington Territory in 1853 and the arrival of its mercurial governor, Isaac Ingalls Stevens, came at a time of virtual standoff. Stevens' three distinct appointive responsibilities—territorial governor, superintendent of Indian affairs and head of the northernmost Pacific railroad survey—necessarily made him the central figure in the decade's tumultuous denouement. Energetic to an extreme, Stevens wielded his plurality of powers with singularity of purpose. His vision was of a frontier transformed by the settlers' hands. As governor, he quickly organized an elected government. As Indian superintendent, he swept through the region with a boilerplate treaty and a short temper, obtained signatures of chiefs awed by his presence, and branded as renegades those who challenged him and refused to sign. As railroad explorer, he lobbied diligently for improved intermountain transportation networks that would link the old and the new Northwests. Railroad exploration, he

reasoned, was not just the plotting of a right-of-way through a mountain pass, but a thorough investigation—the "general feeling of a belt of country"—that would direct orderly and fruitful settlement.

Washington's Indian War

Territorial self-confidence, largely a result of confidence in the governor, received a blow in the fall of 1855, when Andrew Bolon, an Indian agent appointed by Stevens, was murdered by a status-seeking Yakima named Moshell. The murder sparked Washington's Indian War, a series of conflicts that eventually moved west of the Cascades, spreading panic among settlers. The supposed order that Stevens had created with the treaties evaporated. Hastening to control damage to the fragile territory, he mobilized local militia during the winter of 1855-1856, ordered the construction of blockhouses throughout Puget Sound, and established a policy aimed at maintaining separation between hostile and friendly Indians. Friction mounted between the governor (as commander-in-chief of the militia) and officers of the U.S. Army Department of the Pacific stationed at Fort Dalles and Fort Vancouver. Campaigns of both militiamen and regulars during the winter had proven indecisive. Each blamed the other for ineptness. The regular army officers, supported by Maj. Gen. John E. Wool, believed that most of the troubles were caused by whites impatient to assume control of Indian lands. Territorial militiamen, interpreting the Army's restraint as indifference to their safety, redoubled their efforts to win decisively, which resulted in alarming neutral Indian groups. Actual distrust between the federal army and the territorial militia created a second front in which troop movements, the flow of matériel, and strategic thinking itself, were dictated as much by the rivalry between Wool and Stevens as by the reality of Indian hostility. Confusion reigned on all fronts. Gunfire was exchanged between regulars and Indians and militiamen and Indians while charges and countercharges were exchanged between the impatient governor and the intractable Gen. Wool.

The most telling result of the war was the virtual standstill that it imposed over the movement of settlers. Crops were abandoned as whites gathered into tight knots in blockhouse communities and men mustered into military service. The occasional skirmishes in the Green and White river valleys and the murder of several families had reduced morale considerably. In January 1856, Seattle

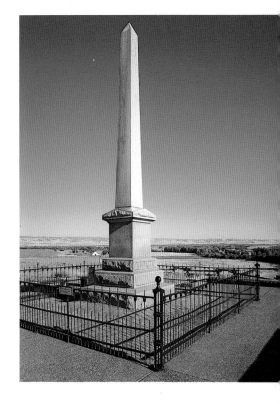

The Whitman Memorial marks a violent turning point in the Northwest's history, when disease and dispossession signaled to Indians the inevitability—and dominance—of white settlement on the landscape. The tragedy foretold of many that would follow, for Indian and settler alike. JEFF GNASS

47

Governor Stevens meets with the Indians at the Council of Walla Walla. Painting by Gustav Sohon.
COURTESY WASHINGTON STATE HISTORICAL SOCIETY

On March 2, 1853, Washington Territory was formed, a geopolitical entity on paper only, for in fact the region still was sparsely settled by whites, and the land itself belonged to Indians. Isaac I. Stevens was appointed governor, superintendent of Indian affairs and leader of a survey party that would locate a route for the transcontinental railroad between St. Paul and Puget Sound. In all three of his endeavors, he displayed ambition, compulsive energy and a keen vision of an empire in the making. Decisive and often dictatorial, he was a man who moved rapidly. Although slight of stature, he was forceful as a leader. Temperamental in emotion and brilliant in intellect, he drove himself unrelentingly. In matters relating to the Indians he was confident that he possessed the proper authority and gift with which to effect the abandonment of Indian title, the movement of the tribes to reservations and the opening of "Washington" to settlement.

Stevens' program for a speedy resolution of the treaty issue was to establish treaty councils at which representatives from various tribes would gather, hear Stevens and his staff explain the terms of the treaty, and offer their assent. In spite of the presence of qualified interpreters who spoke the true languages of the tribes, Stevens chose to conduct the negotiations in Chinook jargon, the trade language. As it turned out, the ambiguity of the language conferred great advantage to the whites. With a complete vocabulary of about 300 words, Chinook was simply too imprecise to adequately establish the involved processes of the vast land exchanges.

The first round of negotiations was held at the Council of Medicine Creek, between December 24 and 26, 1854 near the mouth of the Nisqually River. It revealed a pattern that Stevens would use throughout the territory in his efforts to secure land. Stevens selected as his commission members Benjamin F. Shaw, interpreter, George Gibbs, surveyor, James Doty, secretary, Michael Simmons, Indian agent for Puget Sound, and Hugh A. Goldsborough, commissary. The goals of the commission were several: to concentrate the tribes into as few reservations as possible; to develop farming as a means of subsistence; to make settlement with goods instead of wish cash; to stem the flow of liquor; to preclude war among the tribes; to provide the Indians with the services of educators, doctors and useful tradesmen; to provide for continued practice of subsistence fishing, hunting and gathering; and eventually to allow the division of reservation land.

According to Stevens' biographer Kent Richards, Stevens' approach was enlightened in that it recognized that a transition period would be necessary before Indians were assimilated into white culture. It was flawed, however, because of Stevens' intolerance of opposition and the fundamental assumption that Indians would best be served by conversion to European manners and the adoption of agriculture as an economic mainstay. Stevens also erred in his assumption that the federal government would serve the Indians faithfully. As proved to be the case at several of the councils, Stevens' high-handed style alienated some Indian leaders and gave a forewarning of broken faith that, for more than a century, would follow.

On December 24, 1854, the Puyallups and Nisquallys gathered to hear what Stevens—"the Great Chief"—had to say. In his characteristic tone, he likened the Indians to children who he, and the "Great Father in Washington," pledged to protect through the treaty. The treaty provided the Indians with three small reservations totaling 3,840 acres; reserved their right of taking fish "at all usual and accustomed grounds and stations…in common with all citizens of the Territory"; provided for payment to the tribes over a 20-year period (in goods); and guaranteed an agriculture and mechanics school and the services of various instructors and a physician.

What the Indians conceded in the treaty was title to 2.5 million acres. They also agreed to abide by other conditions, including freeing slaves and prohibiting alcohol on reservations. Reservations were created at Squaxin Island, the mouth of the Puyallup River (now the city of Tacoma) and near the mouth of the Nisqually River.

Stevens regarded his settlement at Medicine Creek a thorough success, and in early 1855 followed with similar proceedings at Point Elliott (January 22), Point-No-Point (January 26), and Neah Bay (January 31). Each went according to Stevens' plan: opposition was minimal and few concessions were necessary. In February, Stevens sought to unite all of the southwestern Washington tribes, including the Quinault, Quileute, Shoalwater, Cowlitz, Chinook and Chehalis, under one treaty. Dissent broke out, particularly among the Chinook and Chehalis, who were suspicious of the Quinaults and unwilling to relocate onto the proposed reservation established in Quinault territory. The council ended abruptly when Stevens angrily denounced the Chehalis chief. A treaty with the Quinaults was later signed, but the Chehalis and Chinook were not included. Invoking Stevens' displeasure, they learned, was something akin to damnation itself.

That spring, as snow cleared from the mountain passes, Stevens and his commission traveled east to secure treaty arrangements with the Columbia Basin tribes. The ease with which he obtained his conditions in Western Washington would elude him, and the controversy over his terms and manner would cause the territory's first great crisis. Following the Council of Medicine Creek, Stevens had sent James Doty, one of the commissioners, east of the mountains to hold preliminary conferences with chiefs of the Yakima, Nez Perce, Walla Walla and Cayuse. Out of those meetings came the recommendation that Stevens convene one large council, in the Walla Walla Valley, and negotiate treaties with each of the tribes.

Stevens and his party arrived May 21 and began preparations for negotiations, occasionally consulting with several of the chiefs who were at the site. The Nez Perce arrived en masse on May 24, with about 500 warriors accompanying the chiefs and subchiefs. On May 26, the Cayuse arrived in a display that was genuinely threatening to some of the whites. With the arrival of the Yakimas, the council proceedings began. Estimates of the number of Indians present vary from 1,800 to as high as 6,000. Although Stevens was optimistic that he could quickly conclude the signing of the treaties, he greatly underestimated the diversity of opinion dividing the tribes—internally, as well as intertribally. The Yakimas were divided under the leadership of Kamiakin, Teias, Shumaway, Skloom and Owhi. The Nez Perce were divided between Lawyer and Looking Glass. The Cayuse, under Peopeomoxmox, were deeply suspicious and outwardly aloof. Within each tribe was represented the whole gamut of feelings toward whites—from amiable cooperation to outright hostility. The Nez Perce were favorably inclined toward the treaties. The Cayuse were not. In turn, each tribe protected its own stature in terms of other tribes. For some, the consequence of the move to reservations would be relocation onto the lands of rivals.

To Stevens, the tribes were either for or against the treaties: those who signed would be rewarded; those who didn't would be punished by gradual dispossession of their lands. Through it all, the dynamics of internal tribal politics was lost on Stevens. Further, he failed to recognize that many of the eastern Indians were experienced in dealing with whites and that their demands were based on a multiplicity of reasonable concerns from actual experience. He saw the Indians' presentation of differences within their own ranks as tactics to strengthen what he considered the concerted effort of a few.

At length, he recognized those leaders whom he could make agree with him. And by conferring advantage upon certain chiefs who were in fact not truly representative, he deepened the cleft of suspicion among the Indians and fanned the embers of resentment among those who would be dispossessed not only of traditional lands, but also of their standing within politically complex cultures. At the end of the council, Stevens had the signatures he desired, only because he created illusions of simplicity in the issues and a false sense of accord among the tribes, and because his dogged persistence frustrated and bewildered the chiefs. The divisions within and among the tribes of the Walla Walla Council festered in time and ultimately led to war.

Stevens' lightning-quick campaign to secure land from the Indian and for the settler left in its wake divided nations and a false security for whites. Conciliatory chiefs became wealthy, their power and prestige upheld by favorable treatment from the government. Skeptics became "renegades." For all the haste with which they were conducted, the treaty councils attained little immediately except to polarize the two cultures that they were supposed to accommodate. The wars they precipitated and the fact that Congress failed to ratify the treaties until later (Medicine Creek in 1855; the others in 1859) suggest that Stevens' compulsive sense of timeliness was not appreciated by the principal sovereign entities he supposedly mediated between.

The legacy of the Stevens treaties is not Washington's proudest. All told, 64 million acres were ceded through the treaties (including those in the Montana and Idaho segments of Washington Territory) and about 6 million acres reserved for the 17,000 Indians represented by the signers. The land was bought at a terrible price for the tribes—the services of the federal government they earned often were useless if not outright destructive and the rights they reserved were ignored for more than a century.

History delivered its greatest irony with respect to the treaties in 1974, when Federal District Judge George H. Boldt ruled on fishing rights of the tribes in the case of *U.S.* v. *Washington*. Citing systematic attempts by the state of Washington to deprive Indian descendants of the Stevens-treaty signatories of the rights they reserved, Boldt astonished all observers by ruling that the treaties entitled the tribes to *50 per cent* of the harvestable salmon. The aging judge based the figure on the words "in common with…" found in the treaties. The new quota distribution had a profound impact on non-Indian fishermen, forcing many out of the business. Yet, for the Indians the decision breathed life into the tribes by restoring the fundamental resource that had built their pre-contact economies. The decision gave them a means to prosper within the economy of modern American society.

The ambiguities, apparently so well crafted into the Stevens treaties to the advantage of the whites, had come home—to the final advantage of the Indians.

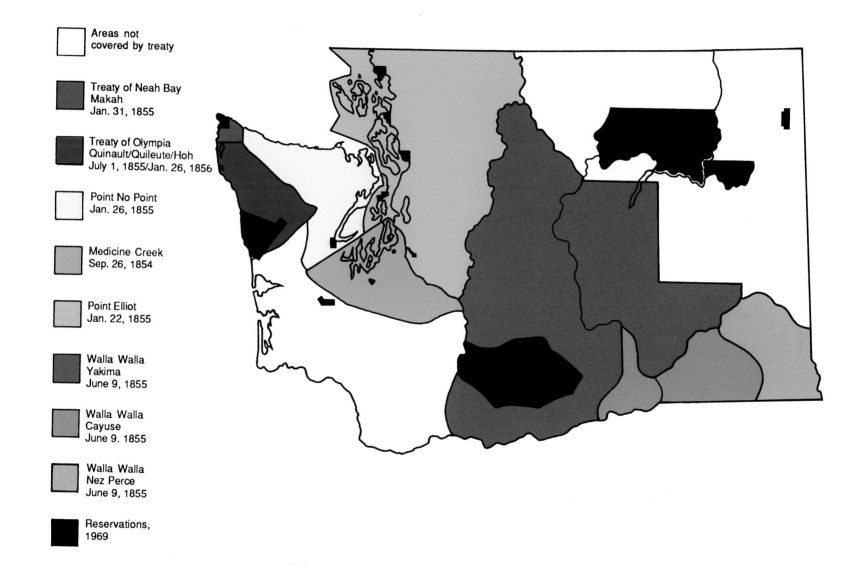

Areas not covered by treaty

Treaty of Neah Bay
Makah
Jan. 31, 1855

Treaty of Olympia
Quinault/Quileute/Hoh
July 1, 1855/Jan. 26, 1856

Point No Point
Jan. 26, 1855

Medicine Creek
Sep. 26, 1854

Point Elliot
Jan. 22, 1855

Walla Walla
Yakima
June 9, 1855

Walla Walla
Cayuse
June 9. 1855

Walla Walla
Nez Perce
June 9, 1855

Reservations,
1969

Pend Oreille Valley. JEFF GNASS

ceeded in displacing the unpredictable volunteers. On August 20, 1856, Steptoe, under orders from Wool, decreed closure of all "Indian country, or …land not settled or not confirmed by the Senate and approved by the President of the United States" to new settlers. Since the Stevens treaties had not yet been ratified, Army occupation would serve to exclude whites (except miners) until the Army was satisfied that peace would reign.

Stevens, however, was determined that the Army's hold over the eastern lands—some of the most valuable land in Washington from an agricultural standpoint—was a blow to his own authority. He ordered a second Council of Walla Walla in the Indian treaty process, in order to vindicate his own position. Scheduled for September 11, the council would include the Yakima, Klickitat, Spokane, Cayuse, Umatilla, Nez Perce, John Day and Deschutes Indians. In it, Stevens intended to grant amnesty to Indians who had participated in "open warfare," but to seek punishment for those who had acted independently in isolated murders, such as that of agent Bolon. According to Stevens biographer Kent Richards, Stevens did not yet know of the atrocities committed by Shaw and the volunteers in the Grande Ronde massacre, and believed that the militia had won a decisive military victory that had succeeded in cowing the belligerent Cayuse.

As the council began, it was apparent that the Indians were not in a conciliatory mood. Stevens' assurances at the previous council had been violated, said the Indians, and events had shown that Stevens was untrustworthy. Although most of the Indians were opposed to the hostilities, the peaceable tribes were alarmed and suspicious of the whites' intentions. As rumors of a conspiracy among the Cayuse to kill Stevens surfaced, the governor asked Steptoe to provide protection. Steptoe, busy building the fort, refused. Stevens then moved the council to Steptoe's location, to assure the Army's assistance if necessary. As the council met, it became apparent that no progress would be made. Although Stevens made no admission that he had erred significantly in judgment, it was obvious that he would not achieve the outcome he sought. On September 18, Stevens dissolved the council and prepared to return to The Dalles. En route his party was attacked and one member killed. They returned to the protection of Steptoe's regulars and finally obtained Army escort for the humiliating withdrawal from the Walla Walla country. Rather than vindication, Stevens re-

itself was attacked, and while little damage was inflicted, the event was very disheartening.

Winter and spring of 1856 were long. Volunteers under the command of Benjamin Shaw conducted a shameful campaign among the Cayuse and Umatilla known as the "Battle of Grande Ronde," murdering mostly women, children and aged non-combatants. Underestimating the strength and intent of the Yakimas and Klickitats, Col. George Wright ordered most of his troops toward the Walla Walla Valley to replace the militia. As soon as the Army left Fort Dalles, the Indians attacked along the Columbia River, severing his supply line and forcing his hasty return. Following that debacle, Army emphasis for the spring and summer was on quieting the Yakima country by establishing a permanent post in its center. By late summer, work on Fort Simcoe had begun and hostile events indeed slackened. The Army again turned toward Walla Walla country, sending Col. Edward Steptoe to establish a post near the Whitman Mission site and to replace the militia. In establishing the fort, the Army successfully stabilized the Walla Walla region and suc-

ceived a smarting rebuke in his cocksure effort to secure the territory's stake in the eastern lands. At last he relinquished control of the region to Wool and his officers.

Returning to the west where his authority had popular support, Stevens succeeded in having the militia round up dissident Indians (and those suspected of being dissidents), trying and ultimately hanging those adjudged guilty. Although questionable as "justice," judiciary processes served to quell the fragmentary outbursts that had characterized the "war" west of the Cascades.

As the Army gained strategic ground in Eastern Washington, resistance among the Indians stilled. The two principal centers of disturbance—Yakima and Walla Walla country—were occupied. Dissident bands were forced into the hinterlands and away from areas where they could have influence over large numbers of their more peaceably inclined fellows. A tentative peace remained until the spring of 1858, when Steptoe marched north of the Palouse in a show of force intended to stop petty thefts and rumored threats to miners in the Colville mining districts. Troop movement into Spokane country provoked the Spokanes into resistance and, judging Steptoe's command too weak for prolonged fighting, they attacked at Pine Creek. Steptoe was overpowered and retreated under the cover of darkness. The Army suffered numerous casualties, the loss of two howitzers and much of its baggage, but retreat was accomplished, and a much larger campaign for later in the summer was planned.

In August, 570 Army regulars and 30 friendly Nez Perces under the command of Col. Wright moved north to inflict a decisive blow to the Spokanes. On September 1, they engaged a large contingent of Indians in the Battle of Four Lakes, inflicting significant losses but suffering none. Wright continued his march, encountering resistance again on September 5. Fighting was less fierce, but the Indians fired the grassland around the Army, which continued its advance through the smoke amid repeated skirmishes. Again the Army's success was decisive. On September 7, Wright accepted surrender from Spokane Garry, the chief. He concluded the campaign by sweeping through the wooded country, killing Indian horses and destroying food supplies—punishment he meted to the Coeur d'Alenes and Spokanes for their protracted resistance. After his brutal show of force, he returned to Walla Walla reporting, "The war is closed. Peace is restored with the Spokanes, Coeur d'Alenes, and Palouses."

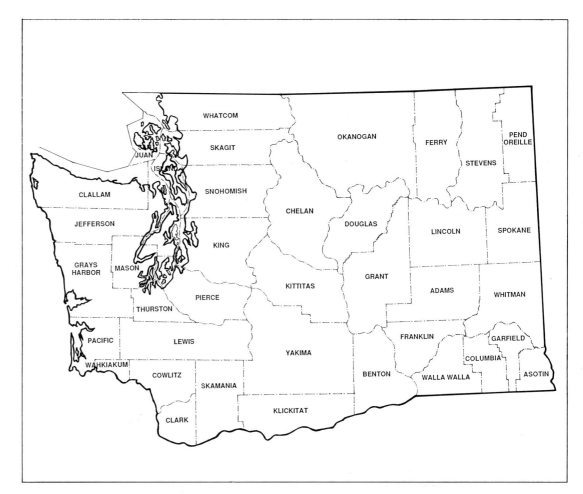

Washington's 39 counties. LAUREL BLACK

Wright's "restoration" indeed had its intended effect. On October 29, 1858, Gen. Wool's replacement, General W.S. Harney, lifted the closure of Eastern Washington and opened the floodgate of settlers. Although ratification of the Stevens treaties would not occur until 1859, the land of Washington, bitterly wrested from its native inhabitants, was open for taking. The winds of contention—race, nationalism, religious creed, culture, economic orientation, personality and military strategy—had blown a tempest over the ripe land. As the storm passed, a new place was revealed, a Washington to be known variously by its dust devils or gray squalls as a new home to immigrants and their Northwest destiny.

Washington's capitol symbolizes a land and its people: Native stone shaped to classical proportions—democracy in a rugged land; Corinthian columns and dentilled cornices carved out of Cascades sandstone, the way a state was carved out of wilderness. Once regarded as immodest, the capitol now complements its setting magnificently. The subdued tones of its sandstone exterior blend as easily with the mists and forest tones of Olympia as with the Cascade foothills of Wilkeson, where the stone was quarried. The 30-million-pound dome rises 287' above grade, a violation of gravity that gives it the stature of a landform as well as the grace of sculpture. The marbles—Bresche Violette and Levanto from Italy, Escolette from France, Formosa from Germany and dark Gravina and light Tokeen from Alaska—were selected to reflect the weighty formality of their office and to suggest the deliberative nature of those who work within. The granite foundation blocks and stairsteps, from near the town of Index, hold the building on its site as surely as they hold a shoe sole in the drizzly Olympia winter.

Isaac Stevens' selection of the capital of Washington Territory was based on several advantages—Olympia had a good hotel, the Washington, and a newspaper, the Washington *Pioneer;* it was situated on Puget Sound, central to settlements as far-flung as Fort Vancouver and Port Townsend. Although the thousand or so settlers who then inhabited the Puget Sound region were earnest in their vision for the future, their reality was that of a raw and intemperate land. Settlements were crude arrays of muddy streets and clapboard or log shacks. Settlers were working the land as well as they could, either farming on cleared land or cutting timber in preparation of farming. What a California newspaper editor had written about Oregon Territory—that there were but two occupations: agriculture and politics—was not even true yet of Washington. The territory's politics were exercised elsewhere.

Territorial government, like most other aspects of settlement in the remote section, required improvisation. On February 27, 1854, the first territorial legislature met, in a hall in a two-story frame building near Olympia's waterfront. For most, the greatest task at hand was getting to Olympia. For A.A. Denny of Seattle, the trip was "two good hard days of tugging at the oars." He was lucky. The delegate from Shoalwater Bay reportedly died of the terrible ordeal of traveling through the dense forest. The legislative gathering was auspicious—among their accomplishments, the delegates drafted a code of laws and ratified the selection of Olympia as the capital. After the legislators completed their work, the building was restored to commercial purposes, eventually housing a restaurant known as the Gold Bar Saloon.

For their second session, the legislature convened in the Masonic Hall, located at what is now Capitol Way and Eighth Avenue. During the session, legislators discussed their future meeting place. Governor Stevens announced a $5,000 appropriation from Congress for the construction of a building and Edmond Sylvester's donation of a 12-acre tract overlooking the mouth of the Deschutes River. During the third session, again held in the Masonic Hall, Stevens was instructed to draw the appropriation from Congress, plans for the building were approved, and contracts for land-clearing and construction were signed.

The outbreak of hostilities with Indians in the White and Puyallup river valleys interrupted nearly every aspect of life in Olympia. Crops were neglected and the only construction taking place was that of building fortifications. Following the brutal suppression of the Indian uprisings, work resumed on the capitol. On December 1, 1856, legislators gathered in the Territorial Legislative Hall—what was to be the hub of Washington politics for 46 years.

Upon its admission to the union in 1889, Washington State was granted 132,000 acres of "unappropriated government lands within the boundaries of the state" solely for the purpose of endowing the construction of a permanent capitol. Debate flourished among legislators for decades on the capitol question. Proposals were made, voted up and voted down, but no action ensued. Part of the problem was that regional partisans from other

Above: CINDY McINTYRE
Above left: *The "Lantern" crowns the 30,800,000-pound capitol dome. Set atop a massive circular concrete slab that rests upon unseen steel and concrete supports, the lantern is unaffected by expansion and contraction of the dome's stone facing.*
Left: *Workers dress stonework of the of the capitol's Corinthian columns.*
PHOTOS COURTESY STATE CAPITAL MUSEUM, OLYMPIA

Facing page: PAT O'HARA

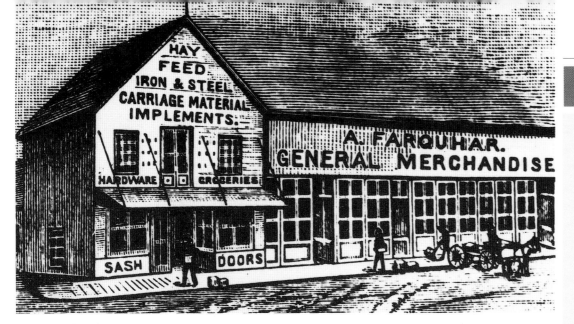

cities—including Vancouver, North Yakima, Walla Walla, Seattle, Tacoma, Ellensburg, Pasco, Centralia, Waterville and Waitsburg—had been promoting schemes to relocate the seat of government ever since there was one. Although on several instances the issue had been brought to a popular vote, the question of a permanent building for the government hinged on a consensus on the capital's permanent home city.

In 1893, the State Capitol Commission was created and authorized to sell the federal grant lands to raise money for construction of permanent buildings on the Sylvester tract. That year, the commissioners selected a plan by New York City architect Ernest Flagg and appropriated $50,000 to begin construction. The Flagg design, selected in a national competition, called for a building 250' long, 150' deep, and three stories high. Atop the building would sit a 150' dome with a winged statue. No sooner had the massive brick and stone foundation been completed than the whole enterprise came to an abrupt halt. In the hard-scrabble economy following the Panic of 1893, no purchasers could be found for the timber on the grant lands and the weakened bond market found Washington's offerings unattractive.

Politics again thwarted efforts to fulfill the need to permanently house the state government. Populist Gov. John R. Rogers vetoed a measure to complete the Flagg structure. In a spirited display of frugality, he suggested instead that the state purchase the massive Romanesque Thurston County Courthouse, a measure to the liking of Thurston County officials because the building, completed in 1892, had become a massive financial burden.

In 1899, Tacoma made an aggressive bid to become the state capital. Olympians for the most part felt that Rogers (from Pierce County) was blocking the permanent capitol idea in order to promote the movement of the capital site. Rogers claimed that he was motivated instead by the economics of building an extravagant home for the government. In 1901, he again suggested the purchase of the Thurston County Courthouse together with the construction of an addition, necessary by that time if the courthouse were to successfully house the state's offices. With an appropriation of $350,000, the courthouse was purchased and work on the annex was started. The legislature was to move in for its 1903 session.

Much to everyone's embarrassment, the new accommodations were not ready in 1903, forcing a hasty search for quarters. Legislators convened in an armory that was attached to A. Farquhar's grocery, hardware, feed and implement store. Although referred to as "the Lobby" by some, it also was called a "livery stable." Many surely assumed that, with respect to a capitol, the Washington legislature was retreating. In 1905, however, they convened in the blocky, turreted courthouse, renamed the Washington State Capitol.

The new quarters brought only temporary relief. By 1909, cramped quarters prompted renewed efforts to revive the Flagg plan on the overgrown foundations on the Sylvester land donation. Timber on the federal land grant was appraised in order to gauge the funds at the state's disposal. Still, there was no progress. A new idea was brewing, however, one that called for the construction of a capitol group instead of a single building. In 1911, the legislature passed a bill calling for another nationwide design competition. This time, a Temple of Justice was to be part of a suite of buildings. Work was authorized immediately for the building to house the Supreme Court and the State Law Library. Thematically, each building would relate to the others. Washington was the first state to approach a capitol campus so ambitiously.

In both 1913 and 1915, bond issues approved by the legislature were found unconstitutional. In 1917, a half-mill tax was imposed, yielding about $500,000 annually. This allowed completion of the Temple of Justice and the renewal of work on the old foundations of the Flagg capitol. World War I interceded, however, and attention was diverted from the matter. Further complicating matters was the death of Gov. Ernest Lister in 1919. His successor, Lt. Gov. Louis F. Hart, promptly renewed the campaign by reorganizing the Capitol Commission into a more streamlined Capitol Committee and assigning

an engineer to assess all of the plans that had been promoted during the previous decade. The proposal recommended was one originally put forward by the architectural firm of Wilder and White.

With the decision, events began to quicken. An appropriation of $2 million was committed to construction of the second building of the suite, the Insurance Building. In 1921, the remainder of the 1919 appropriation was authorized for extending the foundations of the Flagg building in preparation for the construction of the Wilder and White building. In 1923, money was appropriated for completion of the building up to the base of the dome; in 1925, $4 million approved for the dome itself. By 1928, the building had been completed. Although it took 75 years, Washington legislators and executives and Washingtonians they served could finally look at their government's quarters with pride.

Above: The "Capitol Group" as proposed by New York architects Walter R. Wilder and Harry K. White in the 1911 competition. The plan called for the relocation of the governor's mansion (lower right in picture) to make way for another administrative building. Legislators balked at moving the mansion; the administrative building was eliminated. Facing page: The annex of Farquhar's store (top) housed the 1903 session. The old legislative building (bottom) had been sold and the Thurston County Courthouse, which housed the legislature for 22 years, was not ready for occupancy. COURTESY STATE CAPITAL MUSEUM

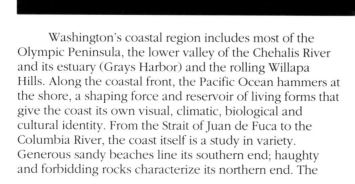

CHAPTER SIX

THE COAST

Right: *Rialto Beach, Olympic National Park.* JEFF GNASS

Facing page: *Broken headlands of the rugged Olympic coast.*
JAMES RANDKLEV

Washington's coastal region includes most of the Olympic Peninsula, the lower valley of the Chehalis River and its estuary (Grays Harbor) and the rolling Willapa Hills. Along the coastal front, the Pacific Ocean hammers at the shore, a shaping force and reservoir of living forms that give the coast its own visual, climatic, biological and cultural identity. From the Strait of Juan de Fuca to the Columbia River, the coast itself is a study in variety. Generous sandy beaches line its southern end; haughty and forbidding rocks characterize its northern end. The coastal upland includes some of Washington's wildest rivers, most rugged mountain landscapes, its largest natural lake and the vast estuaries of Willapa Bay, Grays Harbor and the Columbia River. The region also encompasses Washington's most productive forests. Some keep their wilderness character, preserved in Olympic National Park and Olympic National Forest. Others have fared badly in a century's rush to exploit their verdant bounty. Coast Country reveals glimpses of Washington as its earliest explorers saw it—thundering surf, the dark forms of headlands and seastacks, and dense forests immersed in evanescent clouds. It also reveals modern society amid imposing and vigorous natural forces and constraints— communities begrudging of the economic hardships imposed by isolation but capitalizing each tourist season on urbanites' urges to take refuge in unspoiled coastal environs.

The coast region is divided into three physiographic subregions: the Olympic Mountains; their southerly stepsisters, the Willapa Hills; and the Chehalis River Valley, which separates them. The highest point in the Olympics is Mt. Olympus (7,965'), which is wrapped with nearly a dozen active glaciers. The highest point in the Willapa Hills is Boistfort Peak (3,110'). The Olympic Mountains and the Willapa Hills give the landscape vertical relief and are important in what they tell us about the processes of continent-building and in the way they affect the climate and have influenced human settlement and enterprise in Coast Country.

Four Shore Types

The coastline displays geological processes in the time frame of the present, of daily cycles of tide and seasonal cycles of wind, wave and current. And the variation among those processes is so pronounced that the differences enable us to identify four distinct types of shore along the Washington Coast.

Along the eastern Strait of Juan de Fuca, the first of these shoreline types is characterized by steep cobble beaches and bluffs of soft, unconsolidated glacial debris. Where wind and waves are particularly energetic, slope erosion is constantly reshaping the coastal interface. Crumbling cliffs add large quantities of sediment to nearshore currents, which in turn deposit the sediments along beaches, on prominent headlands and on sandspits that are common along this section of coast.

Two significant depositional features, Ediz Hook, a sandspit formed by river sediments formerly deposited by the now-dammed Elwha River, and Dungeness Spit, which is composed of both river and bluff sediments, are prominent shore features of the region. Ediz Hook forms a long, arcing natural breakwater, which shelters Port Angeles Harbor. Dungeness Spit, reported to be the longest natural sandspit in the world, is a critical habitat link for multitudes of migratory waterfowl, shorebirds and associated predators.

The western end of the Strait features the second coast type. Sandstone and shale formations that date from about 25 million years ago tower above the beaches and reveal fossil evidence of warm temperate seas of the Miocene epoch. The shoreline is irregular, scattered with tiny pocket beaches, slight coves and broken headlands. Abrasion platforms pocked with tidepools skirt the worn palisades; the transition from the gray swells of the Pacific to the gray face of the coastal rocks is a fringe of bursting white water. The pocket beach region wraps around Cape Flattery and extends south to about the Hoh River. Along the jagged Pacific coast, the shore is wild in appearance, defended by reefs, broken headlands and myriad offshore rocks and islets. Although inaccessible except on foot, sections of the coast in Olympic National Park receive many hikers.

South of the Hoh River is a region delineated by geologists as the coast's "terrace" region, the third type of coast. Here, evidence of glaciation is apparent in a series of upland benches or piedmont plains made of outwash from alpine glaciers of the Olympics. The flat-topped surfaces of Destruction and Alexander islands are of the same elevation as the piedmont surface of the mainland, suggesting that the surfaces once were connected as a wide coastal plain. Their separation by coastal erosion reveals that the shoreline has advanced as much as three and a half miles inland over the last 6,000 years. Coastal rock formations in this region are mainly massive beds of sandstone and siltstone—relatively soft sedimentary rocks generally less than 40 million years of age. Wide fine-sand beaches also are common in this region, nourished by material from eroding seacliffs and sediments discharged from coastal rivers. Evidence of general tectonic uplift is seen throughout the terrace region in elevated scour platforms that are etched into seacliffs more than 100' above sea level. The "fossil" boreholes of piddock clams, which vanished some 70,000 years ago, pock these uplifted sediments.

Point Grenville marks another general boundary along the coast. To the south, long expanses of fine-sand beach and associated depositional features like broad points, spits and bars generally characterize the land's edge. Other very complex and striking coastal features of the southern region are the three large estuaries, Grays Harbor, Willapa Bay (Shoalwater Bay) and the Columbia River. The Columbia, capable of transporting huge quanti-

ties of sediment to the ocean, influences the shape of Washington's south coast profoundly.

Grays Harbor is the well-developed estuary in a recently drowned outwash channel of the Chehalis River. The Willapa Estuary and the Long Beach Peninsula also are quite youthful. As sea level rose following the last ice age, Pacific waves lapped against what is now the estuary's

Above: *Olympic Coast, north of Kalaloch.* JEFF GNASS

Facing page: *The Graywolf Needles, Olympic National Park.* PAT O'HARA

the relative calm of the protected embayment. The sediment load of the Columbia River contributes a high volume of the material carried northward in the longshore currents. Even in the historical era, accreted lands along the Long Beach Peninsula have widened because of the addition of the North and South Jetties to the mouth of the Columbia River and the resulting disruption of the sediment movement regime.

Climate

Few natural elements of the coastal region provoke as much uncertainty in visitors and residents alike as the weather. A certain degree of confusion is appropriate because of built-in ironies in the coast's climatic scheme. Although Coast Country is notable for its extremes in precipitation (125″ to 200″ annually in the western foothills and less than 20″ annually on the northeastern corner of the Olympic Peninsula), its proximity to the moderating influence of the Pacific makes it Washington's most stable region in terms of temperature variation. Here, on the average, the daily range of temperature during the summer is 12°F and during the winter 25°F. A graphic representation of the precipitation curve near the coast would show a steep peak during the winter months, but a deep trough during the summer. A graphic representation of temperature variation, on the other hand, is a gentle hump, slightly steeper inland than along the coast.

Isolated or Accessible

The history of the coastal region is a colorful mixture of isolation and accessibility. Villages and settlements occurred where the physical configuration of landscape permitted and, even today, civilization along the coast is largely constrained by the natural forces of the land, sea and rivers. For some, like the Quileute Indians of the mouth of the Quillayute River and the Makah of Cape Flattery, nature provided perfect fortresses. Given a high degree of insularity by the remoteness of these redoubts, the tribes weathered attacks by rivals and avoided dispossession of their principal villages by white settlers.

For early settlers the problems of isolation compounded the task of organizing the territory. Deepwater ports had better access to other Pacific ports than to settlements in the miry, forested backlands. As a result, it was easier to obtain goods from San Francisco than to receive mail from Olympia. Even today, some old homes

eastern shore. But sediment flowing into the Pacific from the Columbia River, driven northward along the coast by heavy winter current patterns, formed the long sandspit we now call the Long Beach Peninsula. As the peninsula grew over the last 7,000 to 10,000 years, the sea retreated. Gradually, the estuary was created, drowned by silt from the eroding hills and filled with shoals of shifting fines in

of the Long Beach Peninsula owe their longevity to the redwood with which they were constructed. The lumber was carried north aboard schooners plying the oyster trade with gold-struck San Francisco. The earliest white settlements of the coast were established by the necessarily hardy (sometimes foolhardy) opportunist who could squint away the dreariness of the close forests and see instead a wealth of timber or gaze upon endless tideflats and see teeming shellfish. One group, known through history as the "Bruce Boys," settled on Shoalwater Bay (later to become Willapa Harbor in the interest of promoting commerce) after their ship, the schooner *Robert Bruce,* burned in 1851. The crew quickly began harvesting oysters and exporting them to San Francisco. Within a few years, they had acquired several vessels for the coastal trade, prospered and founded the town of Bruceport. Their success worked like magnetism to attract others to Shoalwater country, a place where misfortune could be turned into opportunity and wealth.

At Grays Harbor, a young man named Benjamin Armstrong established, with two partners, a Chehalis River sawmill in 1852. According to one contemporary account, Armstrong's mill could handle logs six feet in diameter although "he confessed [he] would prefer operating on three or four foot logs, as he can handle them easier." Like the Bruce Boys, Armstrong had carved a handhold that others would grasp in creating a civilization. According to Grays Harbor historian Edwin Van Syckle, the Armstrong mill cut the lumber used in nearly all the pioneer structures in the Chehalis River Valley.

The coast was not entirely generous, however. Although the estuaries and forests were kind to settlers, treacherous bars at the mouth of the Columbia River and the entrances to Shoalwater Bay and Grays Harbor frequently devoured ships. And farther north, where the coastline offered no harbor, the dark shore resisted settlement until much later. As late as 1855, when Indian tribes of the coast met with Governor Isaac Stevens to sign the Treaty of Olympia, few whites had visited the coastal villages of the Hoh and Quileute people. Fewer had ventured through the forests that arched toward the Olympics. None had penetrated the mountains themselves. Homesteading occurred late in the 19th century, and the only means of reaching the prairie patches that irregularly lined the river valleys was by canoeing along the coast and by poling river dugouts along the silt-laden rivers.

Much of the timber of the Olympics' coastal slopes was still intact at the end of the 19th century, when natural-resources policy took a dramatic change of course. Although unroaded and unrailroaded, public lands of the Olympic Peninsula were open to land entry claims and private acquisition. The Progressive Conservationists, rallying around Gifford Pinchot, saw to the creation of a system of federal forest reserves intended to check the headlong destruction of American forests. In 1897, President Grover Cleveland established the 2.1-million-acre Olympic Forest Reserve, closing the land to entry. Encompassing the mountainous core of the peninsula, as well as much of the timbered coastal foothill region, the land entered into the custody of a federal government whose mission to conserve natural resources for future generations would ultimately be refined by the creation of numerous conservation agencies with a variety of mandates. In sharp contrast to the green hills of southwest Washington, where the very idea of federal stewardship arrived too late, major parts of the Olympic Peninsula were spared the rapacious axe and steam donkey, later to be "managed" in a much more moderate form by the U.S. Forest Service or preserved intact as Olympic National Park.

Roller-Coaster Economy

From the first rowdy days of settlement, the natural-resource economy of the coastal region has been a roller coaster. The glum appearance of many timber towns today represents only the most recent of many cycles of poverty that have afflicted a region where broad trends of home interest rates, housing starts and foreign competition bear heavily on whether the local mill is hiring or laying off and whether there is work in the woods.

Efforts to stabilize the timber economy met with limited success in several communities. The towns of Shelton and McCleary, in the southeast corner of the Olympic Peninsula, benefitted from a historic arrangement between the Simpson Logging Company and the U.S. Forest Service. Under terms of Public Law 273, passed by Congress in 1946, the Shelton Cooperative Sustained Yield Unit established a pool of timber on both federal and private land to be managed on a 100-year harvest cycle. The object was to cooperatively plan and manage timber resources to assure a steady flow of logs to Simpson and steady work for local residents, as well as to advance the art of forest-resource planning and management. Although it succeeded in damping the boom or bust excesses of the volatile timber economy, critics point to the labyrinth of muddy logging roads of the southern Olympics and the vast clearcut areas and bluntly state that the company got the best of the deal.

Fish and shellfish resources of Coast Country also saw decades of boom-and-bust cycles very similar to those of timber. The oysters of the rich Shoalwater Bay (Willapa) estuary were an early source of wealth, but by the 1890s the native oyster had been harvested out. In 1900, Chesapeake oysters were planted, forming the shellfish mainstay for Willapa Bay for two decades. Disease, overharvest and other factors quickly overtook these too. In 1924, the introduction of Japanese oysters reestablished an oyster economy in Willapa Bay. Since then, vigorous cultivation and zealous guardianship over water quality have yielded an industry that produces about $2 million annually.

The greatest marine resource of the coastal region is salmon. The five species of Pacific salmon have surged up the swift coastal rivers since long before men kept records; the earliest records we have speak of abundance beyond belief. But as the coastal region bent to the settler, as rivers were choked with splash dams, estuaries clouded with pollution, the mountain foothills bled of their soil by destructive timber practices and spawning gravel clogged with silt, the natural abundance of the salmon waned. As hydroelectric dams and irrigation diversions checked the timeless routes of return, the return itself ceased. Offshore, the mechanization of trolling and the sheer increase in the number of commercial fishermen spelled trouble for the fish. Fewer fish returned to less habitat—a death spiral that imperiled the whole resource.

Countering the trend—at least in theory—was the notion that the decline of salmon could be mitigated by intensive efforts to raise salmon in hatcheries. From both financial and biological perspectives, hatcheries proved as much a problem as a panacea. With government funding restricted by "belt tightening," certain hatcheries have been intermittently closed and reopened to bring agency costs down. The explicit fickleness of the budgetary process as the touchstone for salmon resource policy dismayed many environmentalists and fishermen. And even when budget cuts were staved off, agency programs and personnel—and not the salmon themselves—seemed to be the endangered resource.

In biological terms, the progressive replacement of many naturally occurring genetic strains of wild salmon by relatively few hatchery-bred strains weakened the overall genetic composition of coastal salmon resources. Critics charged that wild salmon, reduced by more than a century of resource neglect, were now being given the coup de grace by agencies supposedly dedicated to their preservation.

Another event that profoundly shaped the management of the coastal salmon fishery was the 1974 decision of Federal District Judge George Boldt in the case of *U.S.* v. *Washington* (see page 49). The major lasting consequence of the Boldt decision is in the area of salmon management and policy. Once the tribes' fishing rights had been affirmed, their responsibilities as resource managers also were affirmed. Shaky at first, the partnership between state and tribal fisheries agencies grew more stable with time, enabling both interests to focus on shared concerns over the health of the salmon resource. Proponents of the cooperative approach point to the 1982-83 El Niño as a case when natural factors could have doomed the salmon runs without the united efforts of tribal and state biologists. With two sets of biologists focusing on the problem and

Above: *Fishing at dawn.* BRUCE HANDS

Facing page, bottom: *The clearcut: symbol of Coast Country's predominant forest land-use.* JANIS E. BURGER

Left: *Before the advent of steam and diesel, brute strength came from muscles—human and animal.* SPECIAL COLLECTIONS DIVISION, UNIVERSITY OF WASHINGTON LIBRARIES, NEG. 1683

Right: *Marine mammals—here, sea lions—formed an important part of the Indian's subsistence well into the reservation era.* WASHINGTON STATE HISTORICAL SOCIETY, NEG. 139

two sets of resource managers weighing alternatives, measures were taken to insure that the naturally reduced runs were not overfished. Many point to that near-catastrophe as a turning point in "co-management" of salmon by tribal and state agencies—where the frustration and anger of the fish wars between the tribes and the state gave way to cooperation for the benefit of the resource.

In 1986, another historic step was taken toward reallocating responsibility in fishery-related issues. This time, however, the focus was a three-way working partnership among the timber industry, Indian tribes and state fisheries agencies, which was mediated by a private organization, the Northwest Renewable Resources Center. The so-called Timber/Fish/Wildlife (T/F/W) agreement aimed create a process by which forest management practices could be tailored to fit specific fisheries and wildlife management needs. New forest practice regulations assure tribes, fisheries agencies and environmentalists that destructive logging and road-building practices will cease. Flexibility assures the timber industry that in a business fraught with many other uncertainties, tough, across-the-board regulations will not make unsound the long-term investments necessary for growing trees.

Just how far the integration of broad natural-resource policies evidenced in T/F/W will go in leveling the grim cycles of either timber or salmon industry remains to be seen. What is significant, however, is that a mechanism has been built to ensure that optimizing one resource will not exclude optimizing the other. Ironically, as novel as the T/F/W process is, it sounds fundamentally similar to the vision of the earliest conservationists like Gifford Pinchot, who saw natural resources as being inseparably linked and conservation itself as bridging all resource conflicts.

The ultimate question facing those troubled with Coast Country's traditional cyclic economy is just how the region can steer away from an economy dominated by a few precarious resource industries. Tourism has been a logical alternative, and a longtime mainstay for the Long Beach Peninsula, the Grays Harbor region and the North Olympic Peninsula. Yet tourism too, with its intense seasonality, creates only another cyclic roller coaster. In addition, it puts great strains on local governments when the appeal of an area shifts from "let's go there" to "let's move there." Rapid growth has overtaken more than one rural community faster than community services and

"rural" expectations of the role of local government can keep pace.

Aggressive efforts by public and private economic development agencies in Grays Harbor, Port Angeles and Port Townsend have resulted in some beneficial shifts toward the service sector and light industry. With every community in the country scouting for such prospects, however, the returns on such efforts are meager. Tactics are changing, however. What remains unmistakable about the coastal region—through good times and bad—is the persistence of many who stay. Recreational opportunities, healthful environment, relaxed pace and close communities mitigate the paucity of employment. And as those same values become more important to businesses eyeing geographic expansion, progressive economic development planners point less to luring new big industry to the region than to restoring the fundamental cultural infrastructure of the region. Business will come, they say, when the benefits of vibrant communities attract them. And best of all, they will emerge within communities where bright, happy people seek opportunities to make themselves and the communities that they are part of prosper. Washington's coastal region exhibits a potent mix of appropriately scaled communities, like Port Townsend, Port Angeles, Hoquiam and Ilwaco; breathtaking scenery of its coast and Olympic Mountains; and determined people.

Above: *Gray whales off the Washington Coast.* JANIS E. BURGER
Top: *Port Angeles Harbor.*
JAMES RANDKLEV

Facing page: *Sunset near La Push.*
JAMES RANDKLEV

CHAPTER SEVEN

PUGET LOWLANDS

San Juan Islands. JEFF GNASS

Puget Sound: Washington's inland sea, a vast estuary brimful of life, ringed by dipping firs and rained on with Western Washington's own brand of sunshine—the wet kind. To early settlers it was known by a jargon name—Whulge—and muddy Seattle was lovingly referred to as "Duwamps on the Whulge." Today it is Pugetopolis, a region called home by almost 3 million people; a string of fast-paced cities and suburbs packed onto the backs of low, gravelly ridges that run north and south, and crowded onto long-buried tidelands. It's the region that has been Washington's manufacturer—from sawblades to boxcars;

from battleships to B-17s; from softwood pulp to software. It spawned thunderboats and the 747, sprouted the Space Needle and the writhing Tacoma Narrows Bridge. It's the anchorage that holds the Northwest to the world—first to San Francisco, then St. Paul, the Yukon and the Pacific and, now, the Pacific Rim. It's the urban setting for a style of life balanced somewhere between the boardroom and the mountain bike, the time clock and the mooching rod. It's a region of dairy farms, daffodil fields, quiet bays; of self-conscious small towns where livestock auctions draw a crowd; of steelhead rivers that get hot on days when the temperature hovers around 30°F. It's the part of Washington where civilization got a warm welcome but had to get used to the weather.

Mention Puget Sound and you at once suggest the bustle of cities and airplanes, freeways and ferries. But you also suggest a complex of natural resources—salmon and shellfish, a recreational paradise, a scenic wonderland. Packed into this region are all the triumphs and disasters of complex human communities fringing a complex and fragile ecosystem—a legacy of dynamic interplay between those who would not have the place be what it is and those who would not have it be anything other.

The Puget Trough

In terms of physiography, the Puget Lowland is part of a broad structural trough that extends from coastal British Columbia to the Willamette Valley of Oregon. Sandwiched between the western range formed by Vancouver Island, the Olympic Mountains, the Willapa Hills, the Coast Range of Oregon and the broad uplift of the Cascade Range to the east, this depression basin is responsible for the principal drainage patterns of the maritime Northwest.

In sharp contrast to the mountainous chains along either side of the basin, the lowland bears a gentle topography of rolling hills with few outcrops of underlying parent rock. In Western Washington, the lowland is marked by numerous river valleys that extend into the mountains lining the trough. The Western Washington lowland of the Puget Trough is divided into three major watershed basins—Puget Sound, the Chehalis River and the Cowlitz River.

Sculpted by Glaciers

The most prominent natural feature of the Puget Lowland landscape is the complex marine estuary system known as Puget Sound. The shaping of the Sound basin, along with the general lowland features surrounding it, took place during several periods of advance and retreat of Cordilleran glaciers that swept southward through the Puget Trough over the last 50,000 years.

As the Puget Lobe of the last glaciation advanced, it eventually occupied most of what we now know as the lowlands around Puget Sound. The thickness of the ice varied. At Port Townsend, its thickness is believed to have been nearly 4,000'. At Olympia, the southern tip of the

The Peace Arch marks the United States-Canada border at Blaine.
PAT O'HARA

glacier, estimates place the thickness at about 1,300'. The Juan de Fuca lobe stretched toward the ocean, tapering to a thin ice-shelf near the western end of the present strait.

The vast glacier blocked the lower ends of the existing river valleys, pooling their runoff well into the mountain valleys. Evidence suggests, for example, that the Elwha River backed up into the Olympic Mountains far enough to form a spillway over Low Divide (elevation 3,650') and pour into the Quinault River valley to the southwest. Each of the major river valleys of the western slope of the Cascades contains large deposits of clay, laid in the relatively still waters of the glacial lakes. In addition, glacial moraines are found far up several major river drainages, indicating that the lowland glacier proceeded up the valleys—in some cases, many miles.

Runoff from the Puget Lobe flowed southward along the glacier's margins, around the tip of the glacier and through a low saddle east of the Black Hills, near Olympia. Torrents of glacial outwash passed over this spillway into the Chehalis River valley, making the Chehalis River, for a time, the Northwest's most powerful river. The valley, oversized for the present river, reflects the proportions of that once-mighty, but short-lived, stream.

Above: *Tulips in the Skagit Valley.*
BRUCE HANDS

Facing page: *Puget Sound histori-cally has shaped the culture of Western Washington. Today it plays an important part in the lives of many because of its recreational potential.* JEFF GNASS

These bottom features play critical roles in the natural processes by which the Sound transports freshwater, river sediments, nutrients and even sewage effluent and toxic wastes to sea. Their restrictive nature dramatically lengthens the amount of time that water in the Sound recirculates before moving out with ebb tide.

Above what is now sea level, the eroding power of the Puget Lobe left the distinctive marks of glacial action on rock outcrops that stood in its path. Prominent formations of bedrock in the San Juan Islands and on Fidalgo Island show rounded tops and sides characteristic of glacier wear. Their northern slopes often are relatively gradual, showing signs of intense abrasion. Southern slopes are steep, the cliff-like appearance revealing the quarrying of large blocks of rock through the plucking action of the ice. The gentle roll of much of the Puget Sound upland landscape—low hummocky hills dotted with small lakes and bogs—is similarly attributable to glacial action. A glance at a map of the Sound reveals that many islands, peninsulas, inlets and channels lie along a north-south axis, another indication of the presence and movement of the massive glacier.

As the ice advanced southward, it carried with it large quantities of rock from the mountain ranges of what is now British Columbia. When the glacier retreated this thick mantle of sand, gravel and silt was laid down as glacial lakes, moraines and outwash plains formed at various stages of the glacier's growth and demise. The tan and ochre bluffs that line Puget Sound reveal the thick covering of what once was the vast ice lobe's rock cargo. Fine particles, in orderly layers, show how sediment is deposited in still water. Larger particles reveal the sorting effect of moving water. Glacial erratics—boulders carried far from their source and left stranded as the ice in which they were transported melted—show the movement of large blocks of ice or the drifting of icebergs. Layers of dense hardpan, known as "glacial till," *show* the intense squeezing action of the weight of the ice load itself.

With the retreat of the glaciers, sea level rose and salt water flooded the low-lying hollows carved by ice. Puget Sound was formed. In a strict sense, Puget Sound extends from Admiralty Inlet, where the sound narrows between Marrowstone and Whidbey islands, to its southernmost fingers—Budd and Eld inlets. In the broader sense, however, Puget Sound refers to the entire marine estuary system of northwestern Washington.

The carving action of the Cordilleran glaciers formed a series of deep basins that now contain Puget Sound. The deepest of these basins lies off Jefferson Point, south of Kingston, where water depth is about 920'. Separating the major basins are thresholds, called sills, where water is considerably shallower. The most important sills in Puget Sound are located at Admiralty Inlet, located just northeast of Port Townsend, where water depth is about 216', and at the Tacoma Narrows, where water depth is about 144'. Each of these sills forms a boundary that significantly restricts the movement of the water within the basins.

Moderate Climate

The climate of the Puget Sound region is mild, due to the moderating effect of Puget Sound. The average July daytime temperature at Seattle is 75°F. Annual precipitation is generally less than 60″; however, parts of the northern sound region receive considerably less, due to the rainshadow effect of the Olympic Mountains. Mean annual snowfall is less than 12″ in the lowlands. Days with measurable precipitation (0.01″ or greater) range between 150 and 180 per year through most of the region. One effect of the climate is that a lush arboreal cover blankets much of the Puget Sound region, including the broad expanses of urban and residential areas. The presence of so much timber was what drew the earliest settlers to the Sound region. The combination of forests reaching to water's edge, abundant waterpower from streams entering the Sound and the transportation advantages of deepwater ports gave early settlers of Puget Sound a bounty of timber and the means to put it to use. The Sound made a large region instantly accessible and formed a link to markets in California, Hawaii and Mexico for lumber. For New Englanders, timber and ships already were established as profitable and complementary enterprises.

An Economy Looking Outward

Early mills at Port Discovery, Appletree Cove, Port Ludlow, Port Blakely, Bellingham, Seattle, Tumwater and Tacoma and other places exploited the perfect situation and created an export product that had ready markets in booming regions outside the Northwest. In addition, lumber was one product necessary to create the towns and homes of the Sound's frontier civilization. Access to the myriad coves and bays where lumber camps, oyster farms and other settlements had scattered was facilitated by the saltwater highway that stretched from Tumwater to Blaine.

As the tidewater timber supplies dwindled and the region became more populous, logging moved inland. Oxen, horses and, eventually, steam donkeys and locomotives were used to transport the giant logs to the water's edge whence they could be floated to mills. Seattle's famous "skid road" was once a pathway to wealth—the route the logs took between stump and dump.

With the completion of the Northern Pacific and the Great Northern railroads in the 1880s and 1890s, Puget Sound was connected to the prairie empire of the northern Great Plains. Not only did the railroads funnel grain and

produce from the agricultural heartland to the burgeoning Puget Sound area and beyond, the rail link opened the hinterland to coast lumber and goods that entered the Northwest by ship. Puget Sound (and principally Seattle and Tacoma) became a critical connection between a nation that had realized its aspiration to a continent and a world beyond.

The Sound's role as a doorway gained luster with the arrival of the "gold ship," the steamer *City of Portland,* on June 17, 1897. Seattle immediately became "Alaska's biggest city." Outfitters reaped huge profits from north-bound argonauts. For the Klondike gold-rush trade, shippers pressed into service everything that would float. Banks and manufacturers were well situated to supply the far north and profit handsomely. The new century arrived to find the place humming, well situated amidst it own region and even better situated in the economic geography of the new Northwest.

The urge to "perfect" the inherent flaws of geography pervades all frontier towns, but in the Puget Sound region it took on a special form. Nature had shaped the land with glacial ice and a rising sea level, but the product was not entirely satisfactory to some of the newcomers. Although they already had succeeded in removing the colossal trees from the landscape immediately occupied by townsites, developers soon had grander designs in mind. Two features in Seattle that were substantially modified were Lake Washington, by constructing the Montlake Cut and the Ballard Locks, and Denny Hill, which was leveled to make expansion of the Seattle downtown more manageable. Of the two, the Lake Washington project had the more profound consequences because it lowered the lake level and created a new outlet. The old outlet, the Black River, formerly flowed southwesterly to join with the Cedar and the White in forming the Duwamish. Lowering the lake resulted in the disappearance of the Black and the diversion of the flow of the Cedar into Lake Washington. By joining Lake Washington to the Sound by way of a canal and lock system, proponents of the scheme sought to reestablish Seattle's heavy industry closer to sources of coal, along the shores of Lake Washington. The project was on the drawing boards in one form or another for decades and finally completed by the U.S. Army Corps of Engineers in 1916. The project added 19-mile-long Lake Washington and Lake Union to Seattle's working waterfront.

The Denny Regrade project was another case of pioneer enterprise making grand-scale "improvements" on the face of the land. As Seattle grew up the hill and away from the waterfront during the 1890s, level ground ran out. City engineer R.H. Thompson thought of the city as occupying a great pit, which was an enormous hindrance to street grades, and sewer and water mains. His solution was to flatten a few hills. Among his allies in the enterprise was Arthur Denny, a wealthy landowner. In a later book, *Pioneer Days on Puget Sound,* Denny referred to opponents of the regrade scheme in this way: "Some people seemed to think that because there were hills in Seattle originally, some of them ought to be left there, no difference how injurious a heavy grade over a hill may be to the property beyond that hill"—where, no doubt, Denny had major holdings. Beginning in 1902, Denny Hill was leveled using 20 million gallons of water per day pumped from Lake Union. Pleistocene till—boulders, gravel and clay—were sluiced down the slopes in flumes and tunnels and into Elliot Bay. Where once had stood a Nob Hill of the North, crowned with grand hotels and mansions, there remained

a spare plain decades shabbily clad with flophouses and warehouses.

While Seattle had to cope with growth constricted by its naturally endowed water boundaries, the mammoth water body was the medium of growth for the region as a whole. The water transportation system yielded cheap, fast service between the larger cities and between the cities and the outlying milltowns, shipyards and agriculture centers. Farmers in the Skagit Valley could haul produce to Mt. Vernon, on the Skagit River, where it could be loaded onto sternwheelers and shipped, in hours, to Seattle. By the turn of the century, more and more ships were built with steam engines and screw propellers. A class of compact packet boats, known as the "Mosquito Fleet," came into use on the Sound. Running time between Seattle and Tacoma on the SS *Tacoma* was 77 minutes. Workers could commute between Seattle and Port Blakely, the shipyard and lumber-mill town at the south end of Bainbridge Island. Scheduled runs of the diminutive steamers laced the region together and secured Seattle, Tacoma and Everett places as urban guardians and benefactors of the Sound's economy.

Above: Coleman Dock, hub of Puget Sound's "Mosquito Fleet." COURTESY MUSEUM OF HISTORY AND INDUSTRY, SEATTLE, NEG. 5011-16

Left: Even the hills were leveled to make Seattle more manageable as a cityscape. Circa 1910. COURTESY WASHINGTON STATE HISTORICAL SOCIETY, ASAHEL CURTIS COLLECTION NEG. 18733

Facing page, top: Olympia in 1879. COURTESY LIBRARY OF CONGRESS
Bottom: Profound changes on the face of the land included digging the Lake Washington Ship Canal, which linked Lake Washington to Puget Sound. Here, water from Portage Bay is released for the first time into the ship canal. Circa 1910. WILLIAMSON'S MARINE PHOTO SHOP, SEATTLE

Living with the Automobile

The era of the Mosquito Fleet was a lively one on the Sound, but following World War I another transportation revolution overcame the entire country. This revolution brought the automobile, and the gradual replacement of water transport by overland transport. Henry Ford's mass-produced automobile, and a general economic prosperity over the land coupled with severe postwar economic reverses in the shipbuilding industry, reordered dramatically the relationship between land and water in Puget Sound country. Hinterland communities were being strung together along ribbons of roadway; logs were being hauled by train and, increasingly, by motor trucks. The land was coming into focus as the Sound's communities flourished and Americans exercised the opportunities of personal mobility.

Clearly, some regions were slower to adjust. Towns west of Puget Sound—on the Kitsap Peninsula, along Hood Canal and on the Olympic Peninsula—were more isolated than before. As Daniel Jack Chasan states in *The Water Link: A History of Puget Sound as a Resource,* "the Sound was coming to seem less a highway than a barrier." Indeed, although subsequent decades have seen vast improvements in highways and the evolution of a large fleet of publicly owned ferries, the days are long gone when the outlying ports of the Sound were as accessible by boat as most parts of Seattle are today by transit buses. Piers at places like Port Angeles and Port Williams on the Olympic Peninsula, Coupeville and Bellingham in the North Sound, and Olympia and Tacoma, once the hubs of their communities, were relegated to the lesser status of being "across the tracks."

Now the hinterland—the low forested hills, valley bottoms and prairies of the Puget Lowland—entered a new phase of development. Early settlers had taken advantage of the natural prairie lands of Pierce and Thurston counties. And river-bottom land, rich in alluvial soil, also had been cleared, where necessary, and put to use. But the majority of logged lands had not been replanted following the first wave of widespread timber harvest. Fir and hemlock forests regenerated naturally following the appearance of bigleaf maple and red alder in early successional stages, but to timberland owners, the big profits were gone and the ethics of long-range stewardship had not yet arrived. Out of the curious blend

Above: *Boeing assembly plant at Paine Field, Everett.* CINDY McINTYRE
Left: *Puget Sound links the Northwest to the Pacific Rim. Imported cars and pickup trucks line Seattle piers.* PAT O'HARA

Facing page: *Interstate 5, the transportation lifeline of contemporary Pugetopolis.* JEFF GNASS

75

Above: *Pike Place Market.*
DOUG WECHSLER
Right: *Hen Sen Chin, herbalist in Seattle's International District.*
BRUCE HANDS

Facing page: *Puget Sound restrains the growth of Seattle and other cities with its water boundary. That boundary, however, also has been the cities' link to the world beyond the Northwest.* BRUCE HANDS

of timbermen needing to rid themselves of burdensome and "unproductive" land, and hopeful farmers eager to turn some earth already cleared of timber, several waves of settlement occurred in the Puget Lowland.

According to historian Richard White, between 1900 and 1920 nearly 17,000 farms were established in Western Washington, most of them on fewer than 50 acres. Of the first wave of settlers, a great percentage were Scandinavians. When economic conditions improved in the cities in the 1920s some of the farmlands were abandoned, but with the arrival of the Great Depression, another wave of stump-farming began, this time with refugees of the Dust Bowl states. More than 12,000 families settled on farms between 1930 and 1935—most, according to White, in Western Washington and on the worst land. While proponents of the scheme touted farming as a way to earn a good livelihood, in reality it wasn't for most. Those who

farmed during the 1930s often were farming for subsistence and not for cash.

Reasons for the high rate of failures on logged lands hinged on two factors, neither of which was calculated at the outset. First was the fact that, contrary to the impression given by lush forest growth, the soils were very poor. Would-be farmers learned painfully that the size of stumps or the height of the bracken in no way correlated with success for cash crops. Second was the fact that clearing the debris—huge stumps and bottomless duff— was expensive and physically arduous. Farmers who could just barely afford to buy the land in the first place lacked the financial resources to clear it. As a result, many farmed berries or raised poultry or cows—and even then had much lower production rates and inferior produce compared to farmers on richer bottom land.

Postwar Urbanization

With the 1940s, wartime industries attracted rural populations back into the cities and caused them to grow. Marginal lands situated a short distance from the urban centers were used more and more for residences. During the '50s, '60s and '70s, the pattern of growth quickened rapidly with the prosperity of the appliance and aerospace age. Farmland of the Duwamish and Green river valleys was swallowed; the humble burgs of the east side of Lake Washington, connected to metropolitan areas by floating bridges, burst beyond their waterfronts and rail sidings and into the surrounding lowlands.

The natural consequences of the rapid urbanization of the postwar years were felt dramatically when Puget Sound residents began to note water pollution problems on Lake Washington and in the Sound itself. As the age of ecology dawned, Puget Sound was in deep ecological trouble. Nutrients leeching into Lake Washington were creating great blooms of algae and weeds. Beaches where generations of Seattleites had played were closed because of pollution. The adoption of strict environmental regulations (such as the Shoreline Management Act of 1970) and the creation of new pollution control agencies such as Metro (Municipality of Metropolitan Seattle) and the Washington Department of Ecology stalled the century-old trend of degradation and promised ultimate reversal. That promise remains unfulfilled today. The absence of strong coordination among the 12 county jurisdictions and scores of municipal and special-district entities has hampered efforts to solve the Sound's most critical problems. The press of urban, suburban and even relatively uncoordinated rural development has left little room between civilization and its extraordinary demands on the environment, the finely-tuned biological and physical systems of the Sound.

Nevertheless, a balance will be struck. While it is true that the scale of Pugetopolis now vastly overshadows the land it settled on, civilization has not fully overcome the determinism of its geography. If anything, as the limited space of cities has filled, the dramatic backdrop of mountains and the enchanting foreground of water have become more important to those whose fast-paced lives are increasingly dependent on the urban hustle. It is the contrast of a high-tech culture with the reassuringly natural setting of Puget Sound that gives the region its distinctive feel as a place to live and work.

CHAPTER EIGHT

THE CASCADES

Early Winter Spires and Liberty Bell, Washington Pass. PAT O'HARA

The Cascade Range stretches from northern California through Oregon and Washington and into southern British Columbia, where it blends into the British Columbia Coast Range. In Washington, the range takes a huge hourglass shape, climaxing with its highest volcanic peak, Mt. Rainier (14,410′) in the south and the broad profusion of non-volcanic peaks of the North Cascades. For most of its length, the Cascade Range is dominated by scattered snow-capped volcanoes—the highest of the Cascade summits and the youngest of an ancient lineage of fiery sentinels driven by the subduction of the Juan de Fuca plate beneath the plate of the North American continent. In addition to the familiar volcanic forms of Mt. Baker, Glacier Peak, Mt. Rainier, Mt. Adams and Mt. St. Helens, the range displays a wide range of wild mountain landscapes including extensive icefields, deep glacial valleys, fractured walls, lush subalpine meadows and dense forests. These mountainscapes have assumed greater value as wilderness through the years, and a significant percentage of the high Cascades have fallen under protective management as national parks or components of the National Wilderness System.

In Washington, the Cascades can be viewed almost as two distinct ranges: the North Cascades and the Southern Cascades. Although experts vary in their placement of the exact boundary between north and south, Stevens Pass forms a convenient, if artificial, dividing line. Structural differences between the two parts of the range are apparent from even casual observation. The North Cascades form a broad belt of intensely compressed rocks and and eroded peaks surrounding the few young volcanoes in their midst. This maze of valleys and interconnected ridge systems is believed to be the weathered remnants of a large block of "foreign" rocks that docked against North America about 40 to 50 million years ago. Although it is not known exactly where the terrane originated, some geologists suggest that the microcontinent originated well south of its present location. The highly deformed metamorphic core now found in the North Cascades suggests structural maturity at the time of docking. Geologists theorize that it was a small continent or island chain whose plate collided with and was smeared northwesterly by North America. Since its docking, injections of magma have built large areas of very hard rock that has been slowly exposed by weathering and glacial erosion.

Washington's most inaccessible mountain terrain is located along the Canadian border, in a welter of ice-sculpted pinnacles and deeply incised valleys. The Chilliwack Range consists of a network of subranges drained by the Baker River (to the south), the Nooksack River (to the west) and the Chilliwack River (to the north). Much of the rock of this region consists of relatively young (30- to 100-million-year-old) granite that was injected into a jumble of older, surrounding metamorphic rocks. Prominent peaks include Mt. Spickard (8,879'), Mt. Redoubt (8,956') and Mt. Shuksan (9,127'). The Picket Range is a continuation of this maze of cirques and valleys, dominated by Mt. Challenger (8,236'), with its vast glacier and the sawtooth wall of the Southern Pickets. Because of their proximity to the coast, the extreme North Cascades receive large quantities of precipitation. Coupled with high elevation, this factor contributes greatly to erosion—by runoff and glacial ice—and the tremendous local relief that characterizes the region.

Mt. Baker (10,778') is the youngest mountain in the neighborhood and shows signs of ongoing vitality with steam plumes that emanate from Sherman Crater. Named

Mount Baker. JEFF GNASS

by Vancouver in 1792, Baker has long served as a major landmark on the Cascade horizon. It was first climbed in 1868, by Edmund Coleman, a sociable Englishman who went on to fail miserably in an attempt on Rainier. One group of outlying mountains, the Twin Sisters Range, rises above the lowland to the west. The Twin Sisters consist of very ancient rocks containing large amounts of chromium and manganese.

South of the Skagit River, the crest of the Cascades meanders west into a profusion of high, non-volcanic peaks that form the Cascade Crest region. Here the moun-

Mount Rainier, from Mirror Lakes.
PAT O'HARA

(9,200′). This region is one of the most heavily glaciated regions of the lower 48 states. According to veteran mountaineer and author Fred Beckey, North Cascades National Park contains about one third of the glaciers in the conterminous United States. Drainage of the region occurs through various tributaries of the Stehekin River, which flows southeasterly into Lake Chelan and through the Cascade River, which joins the Skagit River.

Glacier Peak (10,541′) lies just west of the meandering Cascade crest. Glacier is the most remote of the volcanoes that dot the Cascade landscape, enveloped by the surrounding peaks and rarely visible from the Puget Lowland. Roughly conical in form, the peak is covered with a radiating mantle of glaciers, which have begun to break up the peak's symmetry into blocky prows, jutting cleavers and broad debris fans. Although Glacier has been quiet through recorded history, its past fury is evidenced by vast quantities of debris that fill the upper Suiattle River valley and by a benchmark ash layer that blanketed much of the Pacific Northwest about 12,000 years ago.

The rugged mountainscape that forms a crescent to the east, south and west of Glacier Peak has a rich legacy of human activity—hardrock mining—owing to localized contact metamorphism and mineralization accompanying granitic intrusions. The Monte Cristo and Railroad Creek areas were perhaps the richest of a wide scattering of locations where the complex terrain saw ambitious and lucrative mining developments in the late 19th and early 20th centuries. Much of the region is drained by long, glacier-carved valleys like the Entiat, Chiwawa and Wenatchee that lead southeast to the Columbia River, and by the Skykomish, Stillaguamish and Sauk river systems that feed Puget Sound.

Straddling the Cascade Crest south of Stevens Pass and north of Snoqualmie Pass is a large area now known as the Alpine Lakes. Declared a wilderness area in 1976, Alpine Lakes contains Mt. Stuart (9,415′), the Stuart Range and Enchantment Basin, along with the tarn-studded high country of the Snoqualmie Pass area. Impressive local relief is due to intense glaciation that has created spectacularly steep valley walls. Remnant peaks are formed from the relatively hard crystalline rock typical of granitic intrusions of the Stuart and Snoqualmie batholiths. The region is drained by long tributary valleys of the Yakima and Wenatchee rivers on the east and by the Snoqualmie and Skykomish rivers on the west.

tains are a broad table crowded with glacier-covered peaks and ice-carved cirques, and flanked by deep valleys choked with gravel and writhing milk-colored streams. Much of the region consists of granitic intrusions into older crystalline rocks of the ancient continental core. Principal peaks include Dome Peak (8,920′), Mt. Buckner (9,080′), Mt. Logan (9,087′), Eldorado Peak (8,868′) and Mt. Goode

The Southern Cascades lack the distinctive core of highly metamorphosed rocks associated with the North Cascades subcontinent. Here the range is composed primarily of volcanic flows that settled over sediments of a broad coastal plain to the west of the microcontinent. One vast structure, the Ohanapecosh Formation, underlies the Cascades and is visible from the Columbia River Gorge to the town of Enumclaw. Intrusive eruptions also have created large blocks of rock south of Stevens Pass, which have eroded to form subranges such as the Stuart Range near Wenatchee, the Tatoosh Range south of Mt. Rainier, and the Snoqualmie Range in the vicinity of Snoqualmie Pass. South of Snoqualmie, the Cascades assume the form of a badly rumpled green coverlet, quilted with the patches of clearcut. Summit outcrops remain conspicuous, but are overshadowed by the looming presence of Mt. Rainier and distant Mt. Adams. Near Stampede Pass, the Cascade crest winds slightly westward, reaching a point 40 miles east of Puget Sound. As the crest undulates southward, it reaches historic Naches Pass and soon is dominated by the towering form of Mt. Rainier.

Mt. Rainier, the preeminent landform in Washington, sits slightly west of the Cascade crest. Its towering cone consists of layer upon layer of andesite lava, ash and debris produced in countless eruptions of the Rainier volcano over the last million years. Yet, the lofty giant we see today is but a shadow of its former self. In an event that 5,800 years ago transformed 125 square miles of lowland into a mudstrewn plain, more than 1,500′ of its summit was lost. Established as a national park in 1899, Mt. Rainier forms both a scenic and scientific treasure—historically, one of Washington's most cherished landscapes that has delighted generations and contributed vastly to our firsthand understanding of glaciers, volcanoes and alpine life forms.

Goat Rocks lie about 40 miles south and slightly east of Mt. Rainier. They are the remnants of an old volcano that thrived sometime between 2 and 15 million years ago. Weathering—particularly glacial erosion—has taken its toll on the Goats. Mt. Gilbert Curtis, their highest summit (8,201′) stands prominently over headwaters that flow east, south and west to the Columbia River, through the Yakima, Klickitat and Cowlitz tributary systems. Goat Rocks wildlands are protected in the Goat Rocks Wilderness Area and form an important part of the cultural

heritage of the Yakima Indians, whose lands extend to the Cascades summit in the upper Klickitat Valley.

South of Goat Rocks, the massive, sleepy form of Mt. Adams (12,276′) straddles the Cascade Crest. Consisting of multiple cones superimposed in a north-south pattern, Adams has been deeply incised on its east, north and west flanks by glaciers. Only its southwest side is relatively gentle, owing to deposits of volcanic debris in its more recent eruptions. Although quiet now, sulphur deposits at its summit indicate that the volcano may still possess life deep beneath its quiescent surface.

Washington's most famous volcano, Mt. St. Helens (reduced from 9,677′ to 8,400′ on May 18, 1980), focused the entire world's attention on the hazards of Cascade volcanoes. Following months of lesser eruptions, the mountain's north face slid off, uncorking a blast heard to Vancouver, British Columbia, sending cubic miles of debris into the air, and covering areas hundreds of miles downwind with ash. What remains of the mountain—a horseshoe-shaped amphitheater standing amid thousands of acres of devastation—reminds us that the Cascades "live"

Inner walls of the crater, Mount St. Helens. JEFF GNASS

Above: *Andesite lava flows, Mount Rainier.* KEITH D. LAZELLE

Facing page, top: *Turn-of-the-century angler.* COURTESY WASHINGTON STATE HISTORICAL SOCIETY, ASAHEL CURTIS COLLECTION, NEG. 2423

Bottom: *Icefall, Coleman Glacier, Mount Baker.* JON GNASS

in dynamism that vastly overshadows human enterprise. St. Helens displayed, in a few dreadful moments, a hint of the earth's forces that have been at work for millions of years in Washington and that have shaped the tumultuous landscape we often take for granted.

Exploring the "Snowy Range"

Seen as a whole, the Cascades create an impressive boundary between eastern and western Washington. They constitute a unique region sparsely populated because of the rigors of season and landscape but intensely alive in biological and geological processes. Rich in the natural resources that fostered development of a society at the continent's edge, large portions of the Cascades now have been preserved for their recreational opportunities and scenic grandeur. Today the range is an enduring expression of wild qualities, which are appreciated all the more because of the relative tameness of modern society. But historically, the Cascades in Washington determined patterns of exploration and settlement of the region. The wall left the region isolated from the heartland of the continent and created two Washingtons, one reliant on Puget Sound for its ties to the world, the other dependent on the Columbia River.

The mountain chain was described in 1792 by British navigator George Vancouver as "the snowy range,"

because of its appearance during the month of May, well before snowmelt. The conspicuous summits of Mt. Baker and Mt. Rainier received their present names during Vancouver's Puget Sound visit. The two summits and the range connecting them convinced him that the continental shore was fast and admitted no Northwest Passage. While in Puget Sound, Vancouver also sighted what was later named Mt. St. Helens ("...another high round mountain covered with snow...apparently situated several leagues to the south of mount Rainier"). It was later in the Vancouver expedition that Lt. Broughton charted the Columbia River to about the present site of the city of Vancouver and speculated that the great river might indeed rise eastward of the mountain range.

For the overland travelers Lewis and Clark, the mountainous horizon was a welcome sight. William Clark climbed onto a basalt terrace near Umatilla Rapids on the Columbia River and saw Mt. Adams rising loftily to the west. Although he was mistaken as to its identity (he thought it Mt. St. Helens from Vancouver's description), the snow-crested range was a sure sign that the Pacific was not far beyond. Wasting few words on the range in the rush to the Pacific, Meriwether Lewis saved description of the Columbia Gorge until the party returned upstream the following spring: "the mountains...are high and broken, and its [*sic*] romantic views occasionally enlivened by beautiful cascades rushing from the heights, forming a deep contrast with the firs, cedars, and pines which darken their sides."

Knowledge of the Cascades' geography gradually unfolded as fur traders entered the country from the north, east and west along the Columbia River. Northwest Company explorer David Thompson surprised the American traders at Astoria in 1811 by suddenly appearing at the river mouth after a long journey from the Northern Rockies. This action prompted the Americans to quicken their pace as they obtained a foothold on the rich fur grounds of the upper Columbia and its tributaries. Establishing Fort Okanogan later that year at the confluence of the Okanogan and Columbia rivers, the Yankee fur merchants began to encroach quietly into the foothills of eastern Washington. In 1814, Alexander Ross, who had remained alone at Fort Okanogan during the winter of 1811-1812, attempted to cross the Cascades with the help of three Indian guides. Although precise geographical knowledge of his route is faint, he is thought to have actually ventured over the divide before being forced to retrace his steps eastward to Okanogan.

Breaching the Barrier

As the fur trade waned and white settlement began, it was apparent that the mountain chain formed a significant impediment. Early reconnoiters of the mountains had proved highly unreliable because of what seemed to be mazes of valleys and ridges. Well into the territorial phase of Washington's history the only direct communication between the eastern and western halves was by way of the Columbia River. Immigrant wagon parties would converge in the vicinity of Umatilla or near Walla Walla, then pass down the Columbia. Many left the river near The Dalles and climbed across the flank of Mt. Hood and then into the lowlands of the Willamette Valley. For those bound to Puget Sound, the journey then continued by crossing the Columbia near the mouth of the Cowlitz River and proceeding along the muddy, and what one pioneer called "miserable," road to Puget Sound. Clearly, a more direct route was needed. In anticipation of a flood of immigrants in the summer of 1853, following the creation of the Washington Territory, Gov. Stevens obtained federal funding of $20,000 for the construction of a "military road" over Naches Pass.

Naches Pass long had been used by Indian people for traveling between the Yakima Valley on the east and the White River Valley on the west. Some of the earliest non-Indian travelers in the region also availed themselves of the route, including members of the Wilkes Expedition, who visited the region in 1841. Stevens sensed that the unity of the territory, from both strategic and economic standpoints, would require a physical link between the east and west sides of the mountains, and consequently made the road one of his top priorities in shaping the territory. He assigned the road work to Lt. George McClellen, whose cautious manner later suggested a lack of enthusiasm for the entire region. Settlers of the western valleys, eager to welcome their anticipated overland brethren the following season, sold road subscriptions and began the work themselves, hoping that they would later be reimbursed from government funds. McClellen was characteristically dour about the project, agreeing only late in the 1853 season to assist the citizen volunteers. The road proceeded at an uneven pace, mostly along the western slopes. Only one party of

immigrants used the road that year, however, and were bitterly disappointed at the real condition of the route that they had been led to believe was nearing completion. For the most part, no road existed. The party relied on their own route-finding and clearing efforts through most of the Naches River Valley and, once at the Cascade divide, encountered sheer cliffs over which their wagons had to be lowered on ropes hastily made from the hides of sacrificial bullocks. Even as the road neared completion the following summer, Indians joked that it was worse than their own path.

Systematic investigations of the passes of the Cascade range also began in 1853 as part of the Stevens railroad survey. McClellen's instructions from Stevens, who also was territorial governor, included orders to lead an expedition from Fort Vancouver into the Yakima Country and investigate the passes from the eastern flank. Finding the route along the Columbia impassable because of spring floods, McClellen instead crossed the lowlands northeast of Vancouver and joined the Cathlapootle (now

Above: *Lowbush huckleberries and subalpine fir.* PAT O'HARA **Top:** *Miners at shaft entrance near Darrington. Date unknown.* COURTESY UNIVERSITY OF WASHINGTON

Facing page, top: *Western larch.* CHARLEY GURCHE **Bottom:** *Stevens Pass summit. Date unknown.* COURTESY UNIVERSITY OF WASHINGTON

the Lewis) River valley about 25 miles from its mouth on the Columbia. Slowly the party inched into the mountains through the winding valley. Eventually, the party crossed Klickitat Pass, south of Mt. Adams and Mt. St. Helens, and emerged on the Klickitat River. McClellen then turned north and entered the Yakima country. While he had "crossed" the Cascade Range, his route could not be recommended for a railroad. He then turned to the Naches, where Stevens had assigned him to construct a wagon road. He noted: "The Indian trail is a very bad one, avoiding the valley and keeping to the mountain sides, where the ground is very strong, the ascent and descent long and steep, so much as that it would not be possible to construct a wagon road along the mountain sides at any reasonable expense." The alternative—cutting a road through the valley bottom—was not much better for, according to McClellen, it required "an almost endless number of [river] crossings."

With most of the summer behind him, supplies running low and most of his pack animals in poor condition, McClellen left the task to the volunteers and traced the headwaters of the Yakima River to Yakima Pass, a few miles north of Snoqualmie Pass. McClellen observed that the eastern approach was gentle, but that the western

descent was very steep. Feeling that he lacked adequate time to fully investigate the western drainage, he retreated to the Kittitas Valley and continued northward. The party climbed Colockum Pass on the massive ridge that stands between the Kittitas Valley and the Columbia River, and passed the mouth of the Wenatchee River without bothering to investigate the divide (later named Stevens Pass) at its headwaters. As the season advanced, McClellen tried to speed progress of the survey, hoping that a better route might be found somewhere to the north. The Entiat and Chelan valleys were quickly dismissed as the party hurried toward Okanogan. Although the Methow Valley appeared promising in its lower reaches, the steepness of its terrain and the close quarters of its upper canyon precluded further consideration. As winter began to set in, McClellen reached Fort Okanogan, then continued to Fort Colville, where he met the exploration party led by Isaac Stevens, which had traversed the Rockies and was entering the Columbia Basin for the first time.

McClellen's apparent lack of persistence irritated Stevens, who noted that "although a very fine examination had been made of the eastern slope of the Cascades, no line had been run by Captain McClellen to Puget Sound." One further attempt to cross Snoqualmie Pass was planned for the winter, but Stevens submitted to McClellen's reluctance, on the basis of the poor condition of the pack stock. With the combined parties abandoning eastern Washington in the dead of winter and proceeding to Puget Sound by way of the Columbia, Stevens gave McClellen one more opportunity to trace the western approach to Snoqualmie Pass—this time from Puget Sound by way of the Snoqualmie River. McClellen ventured to the famous falls and turned around when his Indian guides gave up the search a few miles upstream. McClellen apparently estimated that on the basis of the snow depth in the lowlands, 25' would have accumulated at the pass. He quickly returned to Olympia.

Stevens would not be denied his "line" across the Cascades so easily. As a group of stragglers led by Abiel Tinkham reached Walla Walla following its survey work in the Bitterroots, Stevens sent word that the group should cross Snoqualmie Pass en route to Olympia. Tinkham, highly regarded by Stevens for his "known energy of character," crossed Yakima Pass (north of Snoqualmie) on foot on January 20, 1854. He measured six feet of snow for a short distance. He arrived in Olympia reporting that the route would be feasible for rail. Armed with Tinkham's positive report (which essentially debunked McClellen's harsh estimate), Stevens went on to enthusiastically endorse a rail route from the Mississippi River to Puget Sound. Amid the political uncertainties of the day, especially the bitter sectional disputes that would lead to the Civil War, the Stevens report was not published until 1860. The speedy realization of rail connections between the Mississippi Valley and the Pacific—and especially between Puget Sound and the great Columbia Valley—was, by then, impossible. The Union itself was coming apart at the seams.

The next formal phase of exploration that added significantly to geographic understanding of the range, especially its northern extremities, came between 1857 and 1862 when both the United States and Great Britain commissioned surveys to mark the boundary between the two nations. With the establishment of the 49th Parallel as the international boundary in 1846, both nations understood the limits to their sovereignty—on paper. On the ground it was a far different matter, for the topography of the boundary region remains some of the most rugged along the transcontinental line.

George Gibbs, an ethnographer and earlier associate of Gov. Stevens, served as a geologist and explorer in 1858 and penetrated the border mountain regions from Chilliwack Lake, on the British side of the line. In 1859, Henry Custer led a party across the tortuous divide separating the upper Nooksack and Skagit watersheds. Eventually, parties from both nations established a cairn-studded swath that sliced neatly across river valley bottoms and the barren rock fields of glacier basins.

Exploration continued during several decades of incidental prospecting forays by a host of fortune seekers. Approach valleys, both east and west soon became routes for prospectors seeking the mineral wealth that the mountains held. Passes held the prospect of becoming transport routes, where supplies could reach the remote claims and precious raw ore could be moved toward a smelter.

Railroads Again

Finally, as the great wounds of the Civil War began to heal, attention once again fixed on the question of rail routes through the Cascade Range. On July 2, 1864,

Above: *Spirit Lake and Mount St. Helens.* PAT O'HARA

Facing page, top: *Carbon River, Mount Rainier National Park.* JEFF GNASS

Bottom: *Avalanche lilies.* PAT O'HARA

President Lincoln had approved a land grant of 93,000 square miles to the Northern Pacific Railroad to entice it into establishing a route through the Northern Rockies across the Columbia Basin and to Puget Sound by way of some Cascades pass. In 1867, the Stevens reports were dusted off and the search renewed for reliable routes to breach the mountains.

Taking up where McClellen and Tinkham left off, Gen. James Tilton sent crews into the central Cascades to investigate potential routes that had become known since Stevens' time. One vicinity that showed much promise was the area now known as Stevens Pass (named for John F. Stevens, an engineer who eventually constructed the line through it). Other routes in the vicinity included Cady Pass, dividing the North Fork of the Skykomish River drainage from the Little Wenatchee drainage, and a supposed "Skagit Pass," high in the Sauk River drainage. A railroad line connecting the Wenatchee and Skykomish river valleys was laid aside, however, when the on-again, off-again Northern Pacific Railroad scheme collapsed with failure of NPRR financier Jay Cooke's bank, which set off the national depression mildly named the Panic of 1873.

A third round of exploration for the elusive Northern Pacific route yielded the final breakthrough in 1881. Stampede Pass, a divide at the head of a remote spur of the upper Yakima River drainage, connecting with the Green River valley, was discovered by Virgil Bogue, a location engineer for the railroad. But the required trackage was not yet laid when, in 1883, the "last spike" of the Northern Pacific was driven near Garrison, Montana. While the ceremony symbolically ended the rush for a transcontinental railroad serving the Northwest, the Northern Pacific technically ended near the confluence of the Snake and Columbia rivers. Cars and passengers were ferried downriver to Portland and then traveled overland to Tacoma. The Northern Pacific link united the Midwest and the Far West, but the Cascade challenge was still not fully met.

Only in 1887 was the Cascade crest straddled by rail, first by a set of switchbacks over Bogue's Stampede Pass. In 1888, a 6,343' tunnel replaced the switchbacks, and the process begun more than three decades earlier was complete. Washington's halves were at last united at their middle by slender tracks that entered a hole in the mountains on the east and emerged from over a mile of darkness on the west. The nation had its rails from Lake Superior to Puget Sound; Washington had its trans-Cascade rail route.

Close on the heels of the Northern Pacific was James Hill's Great Northern route. In 1890, a horse trail had been built over Stevens Pass. Exploration in 1890 and 1891 established the site as suitable for the Great Northern. By January 6, 1893, track had been laid, in switchbacks similar to those at Stampede. In 1900, a tunnel two and two-third miles long was completed beneath the summit. Crossing the pass was fraught with its own hazards during the winter. On March 2, 1910, Washington's greatest rail disaster struck when an avalanche swept a freight and a passenger train, along with the Wellington depot, hundreds of feet into a canyon, killing 118 people. The passenger train had been stalled at Wellington, at the western terminus of the summit tunnel, for more than a week because of snow on the track. In 1929, the 7.79-mile "longest railroad tunnel in the Western Hemisphere" was completed, eliminating considerable track with high avalanche exposure.

Highways and Protection

The advent of the automobile greatly shifted the priorities in establishing routes through the summit passes. While most potential routes were well known by the early 1920s, financing the roads became the major stumbling block. The highway over Snoqualmie Pass (3,004') was completed in 1914, following a pioneer wagon road built by Arthur Denny in the 1860s. In the road's early years, Snoqualmie Summit marked the distance that automobiles could travel in one day from Seattle. A narrow right-of-way over Stevens Pass (4,061'), was completed in 1924 with funds provided by King, Snohomish and Chelan counties. Its 1925 dedication marked the "opening" of the Wenatchee Valley to the west and provided motorists with access to Cascade scenery and one of Washington's earliest ski destinations.

The creation of Mt. Rainier National Park in 1899 and the development of automobile travel to and about that natural wonder in the first decades of the 20th century led to dreams of an "around-the-mountain" highway that persisted into the 1940s. Excursionists could reach Paradise, on Rainier's south flank, by horse carriage as early as 1896. A road suitable for automobiles was completed in 1915. Other routes fared worse, primarily because of budget shortages in the fledgling National Park Service. The Mather Parkway, connecting Enumclaw with Yakima by way of Chinook Pass (5,400'), was dedicated in 1932 in honor of the National Park Service's first director, Stephen Mather. The Civilian Conservation Corps of the Great Depression contributed greatly to road-building efforts in the park. The corps surveyed the Stevens Canyon Road and completed parts of the West-side Road, the road to Sunrise and the road from Cayuse Pass to Ohanapecosh in 1940. The highway over White Pass (4,500') also was dedicated that year.

Only the North Cascades lacked a through route by mid-20th century. Old prospecting routes and supply roads wound high into the mountain valleys where mineral wealth had briefly glimmered, but the ferocious terrain effectively barred passage. Transmountain routes were political hay for many Eastern Washington politicians, especially in the Okanogan country, which into the 1960s remained the most remote part of the state despite its relatively central geographic placement. Yet, in the distant corridors of power the priority of such roads remained secondary. In a 1966 report to the U.S. Senate, the North Cascades Study Team advised the establishment of North Cascades National Park. The highway, then, seemed imperiled because of its impact on the wilderness quality of the region. A compromise allowed the highway but kept it free of commercial development. In 1972 the highway link was dedicated, connecting the Skagit Valley with the Methow Valley by crossing Rainy and Washington passes. The opening of the highway marked the unification of the east and west segments of northern Washington—160 years after fur trader Alexander Ross followed his Indian guides over the Cascades.

Washington's Cascade Range constitutes the state's wildest and most distinctively natural assemblage of landforms. In terms of natural resources, it has supplied a large share of the timber cut in postwar years. Its water, originating in the range's glaciers, lakes and gathering rivers has supplied the cities of Puget Sound with drinking water, the fields and orchards east of the mountains with irrigation and hydroelectricity, which has permitted the shift throughout the Northwest from agriculture to industry. In terms of recreation, the Cascade Range has shaped a lifestyle that is distinctly homegrown. The mushrooming growth during the 1950s, 1960s and 1970s of outdoor sports—hiking, skiing, mountaineering—created a huge economy of leisure, and introduced a new factor into the ancient equation of economic progress of regions and their cities—quality of life.

It is not surprising that a metropolitan population in such proximity to mountains, with all they have to offer, has become strident in its desire to protect its mountain landscapes. A hundred years after statehood, and nearly 140 years after the formation of the territory that the mountains so inconveniently bisected, Washington's principal geographic liability is among its most cherished inheritances. Through protection of the forbidding alp slopes of the North Cascades, secured in North Cascades National Park; the remote wilderness valleys of the Glacier Peak Wilderness, formed in 1939; the lake-pocked high country of Alpine Lakes Wilderness, created in 1976; Mt. Rainier, a crown jewel of the nation since 1899; the ravaged and recovering landscape of St. Helens, Washingtonians have established that their Cascades are to be preserved as a landscape beloved in its natural state. For modern society, then, the challenge of the Cascades is the opposite of what it was for our pioneer builders, for whom the range was a nuisance and "overcoming" it their destiny.

CHAPTER NINE

COLUMBIA BASIN

Right: *The Palouse.* TOM & PAT LEESON
Facing page: *Sand dock wildflowers, Juniper Dunes.* PAT O'HARA

From Steptoe Butte, the land looks like a great feather bed, its surface a quilted coverlet of wheatstraw and umber. The green peaks of the Clearwater Mountains form its headboard. Reclining at its foot, a hundred miles to the west, is the Columbia River. Below, things get lost in distance—horses, houses, towns get swallowed in the space of the country. The turbulent Palouse hill country flattens in the perspective, its lively relief pressed out by the midday light. From here, three impressions combine to accurately describe the Columbia Basin. One is its fertility. Another is its aridity. The third is its scale. While the first term describes its promise, the second describes its harsh reality. The third represents its challenge.

The challenge of the Columbia Basin has placed humans at the edges of their successive technologies—the largest teams of draft horses, the hardiest strains of wheat, the new-fangled combine, and the mightiest dam. But even more importantly, the challenge required that government promote stewardship of natural resources for the nation's good, with the farmer as working partner.

Until it was harnessed, the Columbia River was the most dynamic of earth-shaping forces at work in Eastern

Washington. Older than the mountains themselves, the river has drained a greater part of the Pacific Northwest for millions of years. Its broad sweeping bends, its scrubbed bed and the bronze basalt walls of its canyons all are familiar elements in the eastern landscape. The water itself, flowing from glacier fields and gathering into tributaries, has brought life to the land, from the salmon coursing up from the Pacific to the pale green willows of its shore. Today that life is found in plump apples ripening in orchards and a host of other crops in the fields.

The Columbia Basin occupies 22,000 square miles—more than one fourth of Washington State's land area. The topography is of parched desert flats, bunchgrass-covered hills and broad, rolling plains with shallow localized runoff channels dissected by deep coulees. Many of the surface runoff channels and coulees east of the Columbia River are scabland remnants of periodic floods, catastrophically huge and sudden, that surged across the Columbia's "Great Bend" late in the last ice age. The Palouse Hills are formed from wind-laid glacial dust. In places, the soil is more than 100′ deep.

A distinctive landscape of Eastern Washington is the gently rolling "Palouse country." The deep soil that makes the Palouse famous as wheat country differs from other soils of Washington in that it was not formed by weathering processes acting on the parent rock. Instead, it was blown in by southwesterly winds late in the Ice Age and is composed of light silt originally laid down by an ancestral Columbia River in the Pasco Basin. Palouse soils sometimes are referred to as aeolian soils (windblown) or as loess ("luss"). The relationship between wind and the Palouse landscape is constantly evident in its similarity to a turbulent sea. Its lush grass or wheat covering rolls with the wind amid the welter of dune-swells. The basement of basalt, foundation for the loess, is revealed where the Snake and Palouse rivers have etched their deep gorges.

Along its west and southwestern margins, the Columbia Basin is marked by a series of ridges and troughs, massive folds that lie along generalized east-west axes. One theory accounting for these so-called "Yakima" ridges states that they represent the folding of surface layers (like the folding of drapes) caused by a combination of relatively shallow compression and the deeper rotational movement of large crustal blocks. Dated at between 1.5 and 6 million years of age, the ridges are probably related to tectonic events that accompanied the rising of

Above: *Lichen-encrusted basalt, Palouse Canyon.*
Facing page: *White Bluffs, Columbia River.* PAT O'HARA PHOTOS

advanced onto the plain. The boundary between the uneven glacial surface and the smoother surface of unglaciated landscape is located at Witherow and consists of house-sized erratics and other chunky debris ending abruptly along a broad front that stretches for nearly 60 miles.

Drainage patterns in the Columbia Basin trend southwesterly on the east side of the river and southeasterly on the west. The river itself hugs the mountainous fringe of the great plain as it flows from the north and circles to the west. At Wenatchee, the Columbia turns to the east, skirting the uplift of the Cascades. Just above Rock Island, it enters the basalt canyons of one of the most puzzling volcanic formations known, the Columbia Flood Basalts. South it flows through the canyon, emerging near Vantage, to spill through Saddle Gap—a slot worn through slowly rising east-to-west ridges by the erosive forces of the river. Near the site of Priest Rapids, the river turns east, into the low-lying sage plains. Ringed on the north and east by the White Bluffs, the river arcs southward.

Below its junction with the Snake, the Columbia circles to the southeast. Breaching the Horse Heaven Hills at Wallula Gap, the Columbia finally turns toward the west and the Pacific, about 270 miles distant.

Conflicting Visions of the Land

Directly and indirectly, drainage patterns in the Columbia Basin have determined patterns of settlement. The network of valleys and tributaries contains the fertile and relatively moist soils that attracted settlement. And the broad back of the river itself carried the freight of the region—goods necessary for the construction of towns, supplies for those who chose to call the land home, and the grain bounty that began to flow once agriculture had become established.

The social, political and (for the Indians) cultural turbulence of the 1850s had a profound effect on settlement of the great plain of the Columbia. Open hostility between whites and Indians effectively precluded orderly white entry into the Columbia Plain. This hostility was exacerbated by the confrontation between federal and territorial policies. To Maj. Gabriel Rains, U.S. Army commander of Fort Dalles, the whole country was unsuited to white settlement and would best remain in the hands of Indians. To Gov. Isaac Stevens, control of the Columbia Basin was necessary for connecting Puget Sound by road and rail to the rest of the United States. The

the Cascade Range. The relative ages of both the Yakima and Columbia rivers are demonstrated by the fact that the older rivers maintained their courses through prominent gaps as the ridges arose into the rivers' erosive forces.

Glaciers shaped part of the northwest corner of the Columbia Basin. Lobes of the Okanogan glacier moved about 30 miles onto the Waterville Plateau, carrying both blocks of light-colored rock that originated in the Okanogan Valley and massive blocks of basalt wrenched from the edge of the Columbia Basalt formation as the glacier

conflict of visions for the Columbia Plain led to a three-way battle that frustrated the settler, bewildered the Indian and chagrined the army. In October 1858, the army proclaimed its "war" with the Indians of the Columbia Basin over, and opened the region to settlement. Two of the outposts used by the army to control the country during the period of unrest—The Dalles and Walla Walla—formed wellheads from which the flow of settlers poured.

Following the opening of 1858, settlers spread northward across the river from The Dalles, scattering into the hilly margins of Yakima and Klickitat country. From Walla Walla, they moved along the rich and relatively moist bottom land of the valley and its tributaries. The towns prospered as each became the center of a growing region astride crucial transportation pathways. By 1860, The Dalles and Walla Walla had populations estimated at 1,340 and 1,393 respectively. The towns grew rapidly following the discovery of gold in the Clearwater River country in 1860 and in the mountainous regions east of the Columbia Plain soon afterward. While miners surged through the area, the towns fared very well, even though the ultimate sources of wealth were located a great distance away.

Walla Walla, near the head of navigation on the Columbia, was a center for supplying packhorses and supplies necessary for treks into the mountains. At The Dalles, goods were portaged around the impassable rapids and cataracts of the river and reloaded onto flat-bottomed steamers for the continuation of the upriver journey. Between 1861 and 1864, the Oregon Steam Navigation Company ferried 93,000 passengers and more than 60,000 tons of freight between Celilo and Wallula.

Waves of Ranchers & Farmers

In his classic historical geography, *The Great Columbia Plain,* D.W. Meinig traces the growth and development of agriculture in the Columbia Basin as progressive waves of farmers and ranchers spread outward from the towns of The Dalles and Walla Walla toward the northeast and northwest, respectively. The plump bunchgrass of the Horse Heaven Hills and Walla Walla, which had fattened Indian ponies a generation earlier, nourished growing herds of cattle. The rich valley soil lent itself to raising a variety of small crops. As long as farms clustered in the relatively moist valleys, most traditional crops were partially successful. As valley land became scarce and the

tide of farmers moved into the drier parts of the basin, crops and farming methods changed drastically. The number of blown-out homesteads that littered the country attested to those farmers who could not alter their concept of agriculture to fit the demands of the parched land.

Cattle came to the Columbia Basin as a by-product of generalized farming. With the lush grass of the vast open range to fatten the stock, and the gold camps as markets, stock raisers prospered. In the early 1860s, thousands of cattle were driven to the Montana, Idaho and British Columbia goldfields. With the end of gold discoveries, these markets leveled. Through the 1870s and into the 1880s, as more farmers took claims, the amount of open range was dramatically reduced and much of it showed signs of overgrazing.

As markets and cattle range dwindled, sheep raising assumed a greater importance. Markets for wool were more stable, and sheep could use range unsuitable for cattle. By the mid-1880s much of the more arid Big Bend country, including the scablands, was being used by the sheepmen and their large wandering herds, although the Panic of 1893 played havoc with wool prices.

In 1896, the Northern Pacific Railroad attempted to force sheepmen off the open range of their vast land-grant holdings by creating a leasing system for grazers that encouraged eventual purchase of lands the railroad considered worthless. Eventually the program led to stabilization of the industry and gave the sheepmen a head start over farmers who were beginning to discover ways of making the land pay.

Rapid advances were made in dryland farming in the 1890s, including the use of new wheat strains and equipment and cultivation techniques. By 1905, more than 25 million bushels of wheat per year were raised in the fertile soils of what had been bunchgrass prairie. According to historian Alexander McGregor, the region soon replaced California as the most significant wheat region of the Pacific slope. Because labor was relatively expensive in the region, and farms were sizable, large teams and implements came into use. Improvements in design and workmanship of the machinery proceeded rapidly. The first ungainly combine was tried near Ritzville in 1888 and was followed in 1891 with a "sidehill" model with a self-leveling device, designed for the rolling wheatlands of the Palouse. Eighty-eight of the machines were reported to have been sold in 1902. Modifications of the combine continued to evolve in response to the specific needs of farmers of the various subregions of the Columbia Plateau.

The hungry markets of World War I and the rapid development of tractors immediately following the war continued to shape wheat farming. According to McGregor, where a particular wheat operation had invested $1,559 in machinery in 1905, the same operation centered around a $102,371 machinery investment in 1925. Indeed, the 1920s and 1930s were to foreshadow the mechanized destiny of agriculture throughout Eastern Washington.

Irrigating the Arid Garden

The Columbia Basin was the scene of another revolution in agriculture—which ultimately would see the construction of one of the most massive structures ever engineered, the harnessing of one of North America's great rivers and a widespread transformation of the very nature of the land itself. The dream of creating an Eden out of the arid reaches of Washington's eastern half probably entered the mind of every settler who turned its parched earth. Abundant sunshine and broad expanses of available land were two necessities of the agrarian paradise. The third—water—was absent. The contrast between the heat of the bare sage flats and the bone-chilling cold of the huge river that wound among them presented a tragic contrast.

There were those who believed that just breaking the soil itself would attract rainfall. Lt. Thomas William Symons, in his 1882 *Report on the Upper Columbia River and the Great Plain of the Columbia,* asserted that, "an increase of moisture seems to come with an increase of cultivation…. [and that] this change has been produced by the westward progress of settlements, carrying along an increased rainfall." Symons based his observation on a tendency noted along the western Great Plains, which was part land-speculation hype ("Rain follows the plow") and part the coincidence of a decade-long wet cycle.

Hope among the hopeful soon centered on a more pragmatic approach—irrigation. Watering Washington's

Above: *The "combine," which both reaped and threshed, made wheat-growing feasible over the broad expanse of fertile and dry land of the Palouse. By 1920, horses had given way to self-propelled and tractor-drawn machinery.* COURTESY WASHINGTON STATE HISTORICAL SOCIETY, ASAHEL CURTIS COLLECTION 25660
Left: *Grain elevator.* BRUCE HANDS

Corn processing, Grandview.
BRUCE HANDS

By 1890, a handful of farmers were irrigating parts of the Yakima Valley with some success. By 1892, with the backing of the Northern Pacific Railroad, Walter N. Granger had succeeded in building 25 miles of canal. The prospects for irrigating 40,000 acres seemed close at hand. The railroad's, and then Granger's, bankruptcy led creditors to form the Washington Irrigation Company, retaining Granger as manager and extending the system. As of 1905, the Washington Irrigation Company had more than 700 miles of canal operating and more than 36,000 acres in irrigation in the Yakima Valley.

A change was afoot in the federal government, however, promoted by the conservationist hue and cry that natural resources could best be studied, developed and tended by government scientists, public financial resources and professional bureaucrats. Reclaiming the arid west became a crusade, and the Columbia Basin a holy desert land to be wrested from the brazen elements. Under the Newlands Act of 1902, the federal government set up a program to build large irrigation systems for the benefit of small farmers, financed through the sale of public lands in the West. The new Reclamation Service studied nine eastern Washington locations between 1903 and 1905. In 1905, the service assumed control of the Washington Irrigation Company's Sunnyside project in the Yakima Valley, purchasing the company's canal system and the Northern Pacific's reservoir sites upriver.

According to John Fahey in his book *The Inland Empire: The Unfolding Years, 1879-1929,* the years between 1905 and 1909 saw development of more than 40 percent of all Washington irrigation projects established prior to World War II. Federal Reclamation Service (later to become the Bureau of Reclamation) involvement was particularly crucial in the creation of the large reservoirs necessary to provide adequate water to the growing irrigated acreage. The largest of the proposed reservoir/irrigation schemes was the Big Bend. Here, the task would so far exceed the means of anyone except the federal government that the squabbles of private business interests were absent, according to Fahey, because no single interest owned enough of the land to benefit substantially from the project. Following World War I, other issues surrounding the long-awaited project surfaced, leading to a raging debate through the 1920s.

Although the agricultural potential of the wind-blown desert of Douglas, Grant, Lincoln, Adams and

arid garden presented its early proponents with a complex set of technical, financial and legal challenges that flew in the face of the professed sanctity of the agrarian individual. Initially, no one knew just how much water was required to serve farmers' needs, nor did they have the technical expertise to solve storage and distribution problems. Finances were vexing, and parties with the means to build the ditches, diversions and headgates were often those land companies that would profit enormously from the value that water brought to otherwise undesirable real estate. Once the land sold, however, the developer was gone. In addition, under the state constitution, water rights were apportioned under common-law riparian rights that gave the water to the landowner whose property it crossed.

Franklin counties was not debated, the means of water-ing the land was. Spokane business interests wanted to see a gravity canal bring water from the Pend Oreille River, with its vast upstream storage capacity in Pend Oreille and Flathead lakes. Others proposed a dam on the Columbia River near the northern end of Grand Coulee that would impound the Columbia and generate electricity to pump the water out of the gorge and into storage lakes in the coulee. The debate was clouded with several other issues—Washington Water Power, in Spokane, was not eager to see dam sites on the Columbia swallowed up by federal agencies; the Bureau of Recla-mation feared the rival U.S. Army Corps of Engineers, which was planning a series of dams on the river; private irrigators in the Yakima Valley insisted that no extension

Above: *Water meant wealth in the Columbia Basin. While most of the region was irrigated by the diversion of river water, wells (like this one, from about 1910) played an increasingly important role in the greening of the Columbia Basin.* COURTESY WASHINGTON STATE HISTORICAL SOCIETY, ASAHEL CURTIS COLLECTION 21840

Left: *Center pivot irrigation.* TORE OFTENESS

of irrigation was necessary in the Big Bend; and the state Grange organization insisted that marketing existing farm products was needed, not production of yet more.

The issue of immigration became an important criterion—irrigation and access to fruitful farmland for the masses. It was important enough to state officials that in 1919 and 1921 the legislature appropriated money to study irrigation development schemes in the Big Bend.

From the technical point of view, experts were commissioned to prepare studies of the alternatives. Gen. George W. Goethals, who had built the Panama Canal, endorsed the Pend Oreille project, while a lesser-known engineer, Hugh L. Cooper, endorsed the Grand Coulee proposal. Proponents of the rival ideas vied for attention at every opportunity, forming leagues and pulling strings. In the meantime, Congress had authorized the Corps of Engineers to study several large river systems, including the Columbia, for the potential of every imaginable beneficial use. The irrigation project clearly benefitted from the Army study, although in the context of broad use of the river, the Army recommendation not surprisingly supported the Grand Coulee alternative as the best way of supplying the Columbia Basin Irrigation Project. Congress approved the dam in 1930, although President Hoover refused to fund the project. It took a new president with a new mission—the New Deal, with its overt social aims—to move the project into high gear. Franklin D. Roosevelt turned the decades-long crusade against desert into a crusade of social justice that promised agricultural opportunity to a generation of farmers blown off the Midwest prairies by the Dust Bowl and dispossessed in the economic drought of the Great Depression.

Although envisioned primarily for irrigation, its usefulness as a hydroelectric facility emerged as soon as the United States found itself at war. Electricity for aircraft aluminum and the secret atomic works downstream at Hanford served the war effort long before irrigation water served the Washington farmer.

It was not until 1952 that the Big Bend country saw the promised Columbia water pour into the waiting land. As the first phase of the program was fulfilled, 556,000 acres in Douglas, Grant, Adams, Franklin and Walla Walla counties received water. In 1979, the Second Bacon Siphon and Tunnel were completed, adding the capacity to supply another 500,000 acres.

Camps are divided on the wisdom of completing the additional part of the project, known as Phase II. While the first phase of the project did succeed in bringing water to desert, the second phase would bring water to farmland either presently irrigated by groundwater or successfully farmed dry. Again the specter of crop surplus haunts economists. The new round of arguments hinges on trade-offs unheard of during the original Columbia Basin debate: Can the Northwest afford to forego the electrical generation capability in the water that would be diverted to new irrigation? Are farmers who currently water with well water or farm dry willing to pay for the expansion of the system? What benefit is to be realistically expected for costs to skeptical taxpayers?

Today, the Columbia Basin's promise of fertility has been realized and the reality of its parched plain has been mitigated. But the Basin's wildness has been driven into its seams and creases, its potholes and scablands, where irrigation, cultivation and civilization find no access. The land is tame. The great rolling swells of the Palouse are checked with the patterns of crop and fallow, marked with the gentle lines of contour planting. Fertility is injected from ammonia tanks. River terrace flatlands are adorned with orderly ranks of fruit orchards. Center-pivot irrigation machines, juggernauts of plenty, describe vast dots of greenery, visible not only from overflying aircraft, but also to the camera eyes of satellites orbiting in space. The river and its land reveal signs of profound change. Where the outsized scale once made men weak with thirst or discomfort, man's artifacts and institutions now overshadow the landscape. In the hundred or so years of settlement in Eastern Washington, agriculture and irrigation and their institutions have gained in size to the point where now it is they that shape the land.

Above: *Drillers and powder monkeys, Grand Coulee Dam, 1938.*
Left: *Grand Coulee Dam, under construction.* PHOTOS COURTESY EASTERN WASHINGTON STATE HISTORICAL SOCIETY

Facing page: *Palouse Falls.*
CHARLEY GURCHE

CHAPTER TEN

OKANOGAN HIGHLANDS

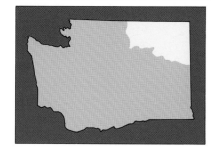

Right: *Nile Lake, Colville National Forest.* PAT O'HARA

Facing page: *The Kettle Crest, near Sherman Pass.* GEORGE WUERTHNER

Northeastern Washington is a fringe of green wrapped around a basin of gold. It consists of cool forest glades that reach out of the mountains into the lowlands of the Columbia Basin, chilly streams that tumble through sunlit canyons before they join the Great River, the out-stretched tendrils of mountain ranges that rise to their highest peaks far to the north and east. It's a corner of Washington that preserves the appearance witnessed by fur traders, missionaries and gold-seekers who entered the country early, looking for the bounties of pelts, souls and ore that were locked in the remote land.

"Okanogan Highlands" is the name geographers give the rolling mountain country of Washington's northeast corner. In this region southern tips of mountain chains like the Selkirks jut into Washington, ending along the river rim of the great Columbia Basin. The Okanogan Highlands are generally defined as that part of Washing-ton State north of the Spokane and Columbia rivers and east of the Okanogan Valley. For the purposes of this book, the western boundary is stretched a little to the west to include the Pasayten wildlands.

Here the landforms and climate suggest a greater affinity for the Rocky Mountains than for Washington's other mountain ranges. Distance from the maritime influence of the Pacific and proximity to the rugged Selkirk Mountains of Idaho and British Columbia give a mix of cold, dry winters and moderately warm summers. It is a region of easy rolling country that closes in as you move north, of lush pineries, of fast streams and gemlike pocket lakes. Today, it hosts populations of Washington's wildest animals—the wolf, the grizzly, the moose and the mountain caribou. It is also a region with a distinctive heritage of human presence, both in the complex cultures of the Indian and the shifting cultures of the American frontier based first on furs, then on gold, timber, electricity, transportation and, finally, small-town and farm life.

As a region, the land differs from other corners of Washington. Although the urbanized setting of the metropolitan Spokane area holds down one of the region's boundaries, the land is the most sparingly populated of all of Washington's major sections. In population density, Ferry, Okanogan, Pend Oreille and Stevens counties are ranked 39th, 34th, 33rd and 28th, respectively, out of the state's 39 counties. The average density over the 11,349 square miles of all four counties is 6.78 people per square mile. This unpressured ambience remains one of the most important qualities of the northeast corner and one reason that the past and present remain closely linked— visually, culturally and economically.

The principal watersheds of the Okanogan country all are part of the greater Columbia River watershed, with a few differences. Some of the rivers flow north (the Pasayten, Colville and Pend Oreille) and some flow south (the Columbia, Sanpoil, Okanogan, Methow). The Kettle River tries almost every direction, rising in British Columbia, flowing south, then east, then north, then east again and finally turning south to join the Columbia. The strong north-south trends that are reflected in the shapes of the valleys and intervening mountain ridge systems reveal both the orientation of large geological formations and the influence of glaciers that swept into the region during ice age epochs. Repeated glaciation has markedly softened the contours of the land, rounding the hilltops

Above: *Homestead, Pend Oreille County. Date unknown.* COURTESY EASTERN WASHINGTON STATE HISTORICAL SOCIETY

Facing page, top: *Near Bossburg, in the Columbia River Valley.*
GEORGE WUERTHNER
Bottom: *Near Dixie.* PAT O'HARA

into worn domes and ridges, and filling the valleys with the sand and gravel of glacial outwash.

Voyageurs to Prospectors

The mountainous region of the Okanogan first was penetrated by whites via the Columbia River, the great highway into the Northwest. The foundations of fur economy were untamed land, abundant wildlife and healthy, cooperative Indians who did the lion's share of the trapping. By the time Joint Occupancy with the British ended in 1846, the ecological balance of the fur trade had shifted. Disease had disrupted Indian populations and beaver had become scarce. The shifting political winds signaled the end of the fur-company era and the beginning of one antithetical to its rough-hewn manner of living with the land.

Okanogan country was spared the brunt of the Great Migration. Westbound pioneers who trekked over the

Oregon Trail were headed for lush valleys like the Willamette and Walla Walla, where the destiny of a tiller was the breaking of deep sod. But it was only a matter of time before other developments put the mountainous region on the map. When word of gold in the Colville vicinity spread in 1855, the region was wracked by waves of argonauts and the hordes of camp followers they attracted. The throngs that dissipated after the California gold rush quickly and boisterously reconvened in this corner of the Northwest and later spread into adjacent mountainous districts of British Columbia, Idaho and Montana.

The Colville discovery came at a time critical to negotiation of the Stevens treaties. While the smaller Indian tribes scattered throughout the mountain valleys of the Okanogan country had been relatively insulated from settlement pressures of whites in the Walla Walla Valley and other areas, gold fever quickly placed them in direct competition with the miners and their hurly-burly version of civilization. Miners took as their right not only the mineral wealth of the land, but also its timber and game. Indian title to the land and its resources was nonexistent in their eyes. The profligacy of the camps, where dissipation and licentiousness were de rigueur, did little to either reassure the Indians that the whites would honor their land claims or exemplify the virtues that the Indians were asked to learn. In northeast Washington, as elsewhere in the West, the mineral wealth of the mountains would repeatedly be used as the pretext for reducing the size of the reservations. Mineral entry on Indian lands, even when forbidden by law, occurred because the lure of wealth was impossible to harness in desperate men with gold in their eyes.

Mining-camp society did have some redeeming characteristics, however. Principal among these was the rapid development of social order within the communities. With the rapid accumulation of wealth came the need to protect it through standards for claim description and property ownership—and other provisions aimed at curbing general lawlessness. Mining camps engendered bootstrap self-government, and from this, town and city governments sprang. The evolution from vigilance committee to town council occurred rapidly. Many of the small towns of Okanogan country followed just such a path in their founding. And while gamblers and prostitutes formed a large constituency, blacksmiths, merchants, teamsters, doctors and lawyers also played important roles. Their contributions were lasting, creating foundations on which permanent communities would blossom. Transportation networks evolved to get goods to the mines and minerals out. Generally, the region opened as ferries and bridges spanned the rivers, and trails and wagon roads penetrated the wilderness.

Following the earliest discoveries of placer gold along the river banks, activity moved elsewhere, particularly into the Clearwater country of Idaho and into the nearby mountain districts of what is now British Columbia. In the Okanogan Highlands, approximately 1,500 Chinese workers, prohibited by law from staking claims themselves, gleaned the river banks for decades following the general exodus from the early sites. Between the tumultuous 1850s and the 1890s, when the fervor of mineral discovery again visited the region, settlers consolidated their meager gains. Freight haulers and merchants who had prospered during the gold rush served newer immigrants who sought farmland in the narrow valleys. Transportation improved both on and across the rivers.

A Forced Confederation

Even in this vast land, conflicts with Indian people materialized early. In the process of establishing treaties with other tribes of Washington Territory, officials ignored the scattered bands of Indians of the north, perhaps because these were eclipsed in perceived importance by the Yakima, Cayuse and Nez Perce, whose homelands straddled the migration routes of the Columbia Basin. Gov. Stevens appeared concerned about negotiations with the Spokane and Columbia tribes only when it became a strategic matter during hostilities with the Yakima. His goal clearly was to keep the northern tribes from harboring or joining the warring parties. A council with the Spokane convened in 1856, but treaties were not signed or reservations delegated. Rather, the pressing matters of the growing Yakima war allowed only a few brief sessions at which assurances of continued peace in the north were traded. Later, in 1858, when terms of that tenuous agreement were breached with the advance of federal troops into Spokane country, the Spokanes and Coeur d'Alenes were brutally chastised. Thus, the northern tribes learned that the isolation of their lands offered them no real sanctuary.

101

Above: Outdoor recreationists atop
Mount Spokane. Circa 1912.
Right: Consolidated Lumber Company
log train, Stevens County. Circa 1910.

It was not until 1872 that a reservation was established for the loose confederation of northern tribes. The first reservation, located east of the Columbia River, was established in April of that year by presidential proclamation. A few months later, that order was superceded by another that established a reservation on the west side of the river, extending between the Canadian border on the north, the Columbia River on the east and south and the Okanogan River on the west. Within this reservation, all of the northern tribes—the Nespelems, Colvilles, Sanpoils, Okanogans, Methow, Entiats, Wenatchees and, later, the Nez Perce—were assigned. Not only were tribal and territorial distinctions blurred in the move, but broad linguistic affinities also were disregarded, and intertribal political factions led to intense discord. In 1885, Chief Joseph and a band of Nez Perce who had been exiled in Oklahoma following defeat in the famous march toward Canada were relocated in the Nespelem Valley of the reservation. It was as near to their beloved Wallowa Valley as they would be allowed to live. Joseph's last years were spent in northern Washington and the reluctant Nez Perce presence on the reservation added another element of frustration and disharmony to the clash of politics and culture of the reservation.

In 1891, the reservation was partitioned and the northern half—1.5 million acres—sold to the United States, which restored it to the public domain. In 1896, the north half was opened to mineral entry, ushering in an era when the phrase "to the north half" reverberated from the lips of waves of new fortune-hungry miners. Three years later, the south half was likewise opened to mineral entry. The tribes relinquished title to the majority of the south-half reservation lands to the United States in 1905. The following year each person assigned to the reservation was granted 80 acres, and the remainder of the south half was opened to sale as surplus lands. It was not until 1934 that sale of the lands by the U.S. government was stopped, and not until 1956 that the undisposed lands (818,000 acres) were restored to the Confederated Tribes. Thus, in just a few years, lands originally amounting to nearly half of Okanogan Country that had been set aside for Indian people were legally and illegally removed from their control. In addition, federal mismanagement of resources held in trust, and the loss of the entire salmon resource upstream from Grand Coulee Dam, represented gross intrusions on the means of subsistence that the reservations were supposed to protect.

The opening of the north half signaled the second great mineral rush to Okanogan Country and the one that left the most permanent imprint on the land. It was more than a rush to the streambanks and gullies in search of loose glitter; it was the era of mechanized mineral extraction—hardrock mining, rail transport, milling, concentrating and smelting. Its towns were company towns—for either mining companies or sawmills that provided mine and trestle timbers for the industrial growth of the region. The towns were places like Orient, established near the site of the "Never Tell Mine," and Godfrey, built around the site chosen by the Enterprise Lumber Company in 1904 for its sawmill.

Wild and Self-Sufficient

Today's Okanogan Country continues to reflect the various themes that have intertwined to form its history. Its industries remain those that have turned mineral and timber resources into raw materials shipped to places where they become finished products. Farms dot the narrow valleys with hayfields and orchards. Shaggy winter ponies graze in broad pastures. Log trucks whine off dusty, numbered Forest Service roads and onto open highways. Smelter dust cloaks the forests near Metaline Falls. On the 1.3-million-acre Colville Reservation, the complex social, political and economic issues of reservation life continue to simmer. Small towns like Republic, Kettle Falls and Colville sport ancient brick and frame houses "downtown" and supermarkets at the edge.

Throughout its history the region has endured isolation. During the early generations of its settlement, its vastness promoted a peculiar self-sufficiency. Its Indians thrived in a region abundant with salmon, game and open space. Fur traders exploited its richness of furs and its river highways. Prospectors endured the quiet of its canyons for a fleeting taste of fortune. Its towns and farms relied on the closeness of like-thinking people to offset remoteness from distant centers of civilization.

The wildness of Washington's northeast country— the Okanogan Highland—is today one of its most valuable qualities. That isolation has its rewards. Stretching from the Pasayten wildlands on the west to the Salmo in the east—from the Cascade mountains to the Selkirks—the wild areas of this mountainous country hold

Farm near Colville. PAT O'HARA

their own and draw outsiders to them. And just as the ruggedness and isolation of the land has directly shaped all previous human enterprise, those factors combine to create another resource of great value in contemporary Pacific Northwest society—the opportunity for outdoor recreation. Visitors on the Colville National Forest during 1986 totaled 950,000, many of whom were drawn by the region's renowned fishing, hunting, boating, hiking and winter sports. Residents pride themselves on the land that surrounds them—rich in history, rich in natural resources and well removed from the tempests of urban life.

JANIS E. BURGER

Bibliography

Abbott, Newton Carl and Fred E. Carver. *The Evolution of Washington Counties.* Yakima: Yakima Valley Genealogical Society and Klickitat County Historical Society, 1978.

Allen, John Eliot, Marjorie Burns and Sam C. Sargent. *Cataclysms on the Columbia.* Portland: Timber Press, 1986.

Alt, David D., and Donald W. Hyndman. *Roadside Geology of Washington.* Missoula: Mountain Press Publishing Co., 1984.

American Friends Service Committee. *Uncommon Controversy: Fishing Rights of the Muckleshoot, Puyallup, and Nisqually Indians.* Seattle and London: University of Washington Press, 1975.

Bancroft, Hubert Howe. *History of the Northwest Coast,* Volumes I & II. New York: The Bancroft Company, 1900.

Beckey, Fred. *Cascade Alpine Guide, Climbing and High Routes: Columbia River to Stevens Pass.* Seattle: The Mountaineers, 1973.

Beckey, Fred. *Cascade Alpine Guide, Climbing and High Routes: Rainy Pass to Fraser River.* Seattle: The Mountaineers, 1981.

Beckey, Fred. *Cascade Alpine Guide, Climbing and High Routes: Stevens Pass to Rainy Pass.* Seattle: The Mountaineers, 1977.

Bergland, Eric O. *Summary Prehistory and Ethnography of Olympic National Park, Washington.* Division of Cultural Resources, Pacific Northwest Region, National Park Service: Seattle, 1983.

Borden, Charles E. "Peopling and Early Cultures of the Pacific Northwest: a View from British Columbia, Canada." *Science,* Vol. 203, Number 4384 (1979), pp. 963-971.

Brown, Bruce. *Mountain in the Clouds: A Search for the Wild Salmon.* New York: Simon & Schuster, 1982.

Chasan, Daniel Jack. *The Water Link: A History of Puget Sound as a Resource.* Seattle: Washington Sea Grant Program, University of Washington, 1981.

Chatters, James, et al. *Human Adaptation Along the Columbia River, 4700-1600 BP.: A Report of Test Excavation at River Mile 590, North Central Washington.* Central Washington University Occasional Paper No. 1, Ellensburg: Central Washington University,1984.

Coues, Elliott, ed. *The History of the Lewis and Clark Expedition,* Vols. II & III. New York: Dover Publications.

Daubenmire, R. *Steppe Vegetation of Washington.* Washington Agricultural Experimental Station Technical Bulletin 62. Portland: 1970.

Edwards, G. Thomas, and Carlos A. Schwantes. *Experiences in a Promised Land: Essays in Pacific Northwest History.* Seattle and London: University of Washington Press, 1986.

Fahey, John. *The Inland Empire: Unfolding Years, 1879-1929.* Seattle and London: University of Washington Press, 1986.

Franklin, Jerry F., and C. T. Dyrness. *Natural Vegetation of Oregon and Washington. Pacific Northwest Forest and Range Experiment Station General Technical Report PNW-8.* Portland: 1973.

Greenberg, Joseph H. *Language in the Americas.* Stanford: Stanford University Press, 1987.

Hitchman, Robert. *Place Names of Washington.* Tacoma: Washington State Historical Society, 1985.

Johannsen, Robert W. *Frontier Politics on the Eve of the Civil War.* Seattle and London: University of Washington Press, 1955.

Leonhardy, Frank C., and David G. Rice. "A Proposed Culture Typology for the Lower Snake River Region, Southeastern Washington." *Northwest Anthropological Research Notes,* Vol. 4, No. 1 (1970), pp. 1-29.

Meany, Edmond S. *History of the State of Washington, Revised.* New York: The Macmillan Company, 1941.

Meany, Edmond S. *Vancouver's Discovery of Puget Sound.* Portland: Binfords & Mort, 1957.

Meeker, Ezra. *Pioneer Reminiscences of Puget Sound.* Seattle: Lowman & Hanford, 1905.

Meeker, Ezra. *The Tragedy of Leschi.* Seattle: Lowman & Hanford, 1905.

Meinig, D. W. *The Great Columbia Plain: A Historical Geography, 1805-1910.* Seattle and London: University of Washington Press, 1968.

Morgan, Murray. *The Last Wilderness.* Seattle and London: University of Washington Press, 1955.

Newcombe, C. F., ed. *Menzies' Journal of Vancouver's Voyage, April to October, 1792.* Victoria: Archives of British Columbia, 1923.

Price, A. Grenfell, ed. *The Explorations of Captain James Cook in the Pacific as Told by Selections of His Own Journals 1768-1779.* New York: Dover Publications, 1971.

Relander, Click. *Drummers and Dreamers.* Caldwell: The Caxton Press, 1956.

Richards, Kent D. *Isaac I. Stevens: Young Man in a Hurry.* Provo: Brigham Young University Press, 1979.

Ruby, Robert H., and John A. Brown. *A Guide to the Indian Tribes of the Pacific Northwest.* Norman and London: University of Oklahoma Press, 1986.

Schalk, Randall F., et al. *An Archaeological Survey of the Priest Rapids Reservoir, 1981.* Project Report 12, Laboratory of Archaeology and History, Washington State University. Pullman: Washington State University, 1982.

Schalk, Randall F. "Estimating Salmon and Steelhead Usage in the Columbia Basin Before 1850: An Anthropological Perspective." *The Northwest Environmental Journal,* Vol. 2, No. 2 (1986) pp. 1-29.

Steelquist, Robert U. *Washington Mountain Ranges.* Helena: American Geographic Publishing, 1986.

Steelquist, Robert U. *Washington's Coast.* Helena: American Geographic Publishing, 1987.

Stevens, Isaac I. *Reports of Explorations and Surveys to Ascertain the Most Practicable and Economical Route for a Railroad from the Mississippi River to the Pacific Ocean, 1853-1855,* Vols. X and XII, Book II. Washington: Thos. Ford, Printer, 1860.

Swan, James G. *The Northwest Coast or, Three Years' Residence in Washington Territory.* Seattle and London: University of Washington Press, 1972.

Tabor, Rowland W. *Guide to the Geology of Olympic National Park.* Seattle and London: University of Washington Press, 1975.

Terich, Thomas A., and Maurice L. Schwartz. "A Geomorphic Classification of Washington State's Pacific Coast." *Shore and Beach,* Vol. 49, No. 3, (1981), pp. 21-27.

Van Syckle, Edwin. *They Tried To Cut It All.* Seattle: Pacific Search Press, 1980.

Van Syckle, Edwin. *The River Pioneers: Early Days on Grays Harbor.* Seattle: Pacific Search Press, 1982.